BestMasters

Springer awards „BestMasters" to the best master's theses which have been completed at renowned universities in Germany, Austria, and Switzerland.

The studies received highest marks and were recommended for publication by supervisors. They address current issues from various fields of research in natural sciences, psychology, technology, and economics.

The series addresses practitioners as well as scientists and, in particular, offers guidance for early stage researchers.

Hannah Genheimer

Fear and Anxiety in Virtual Reality

Investigations of cue and context conditioning in virtual environment

 Springer

Hannah Genheimer
Würzburg, Germany

BestMasters
ISBN 978-3-658-08202-4   ISBN 978-3-658-08203-1 (eBook)
DOI 10.1007/978-3-658-08203-1

Library of Congress Control Number: 2014956936

Printed on acid-free paper

Springer is a brand of Springer Fachmedien Wiesbaden
Springer Fachmedien Wiesbaden is part of Springer Science+Business Media
(www.springer.com)

Preface

This interdisciplinary master thesis combines biological and psychological research. The study was implemented at the University of Würzburg in the Department of Psychology I (Biological Psychology, Clinical Psychology, and Psychotherapy).

Our department includes research groups focusing on experimental clinical psychology, affective neuroscience, clinical psychophysiology, imitation behavior, eating behavior, cardiopsychology and fMRI, associative learning and virtual reality research.

Our research tracks are two-fold: The biopsychological and experimental research addresses basic as well as application-oriented questions. The latter refers mainly to the field of clinical psychology.

One focus is directed towards emotional and motivational phenomena such as anxiety, pain, substance abuse, and addiction. Here, we examine the underlying behavioral and psychophysiological mechanisms in healthy and clinical samples using various study designs and methods. Furthermore, we investigate the physiological basis of social perception, verbal communication and interaction (Social Cognitive Neuroscience).

A very special methodological feature at our department is the research in virtual environments (computer simulations) in order to induce and measure affective states in humans. Within the applied research, we investigate the efficacy of exposure in virtual environments for the therapy of different phobias (flight phobia, tunnel phobia, spider phobia, height phobia, social phobia) as well as the essential components for treatment efficacy. In basic research we examine the psychophysiological and neuropsychological correlates of stress, fear and nausea. Dependent measures include beside subjective data physiological measures such as heart rate, skin conductance, facial muscle activity (EMG), blood pressure, respiration, and startle response. To measure brain activity we apply EEG and fMRI technology.

The study presented in this book combines the advantages of virtual reality and the research on neurophysiological and behavioral mechanisms of experimentally induced fear and anxiety. Eventually, the research will help to understand basic mechanisms in the development of fear and anxiety disorders.

Prof. Dr. Paul Pauli   Prof. Dr. Matthias Wieser

Acknowledgements

Conducting this master thesis was very enjoyable and demanding in the kind and boosting atmosphere at the department of psychology. Many people supported me during this work and earn my special gratitude:

Thank you very much

Dr. Evelyn Glotzbach-Schoon
... for your fantastic supervision of this master thesis. You supported me with your help and advice at best and at any time.

Prof. Dr. Andreas Mühlberger
... for your great research idea, critical remarks and especially for the enablement of this work despite your move to Regensburg.

Prof. Dr. Paul Pauli
... for encouraging my work at the institute and the always very helpful discussions.

Prof. Dr. Matthias Wieser
... for your help with the EEG in this study. Special thanks for getting me enthusiastic about science and for the fabulous dedicated supervision during 4 years.

Prof. Dr. Wolfgang Rössler
... for unproblematic and smart supervision of this master thesis on behalf of biology.

the whole fear and anxiety-workgroup
... for your kind help, the fruitful discussions and new suggestions.

all subjects
... for your courageous participation in the pilot study as well as in the main experiment.

my girls from Würzburg
... for many wonderful and unforgettable evenings with you. Many thanks for your hardworking shared proofreading and all the helpful comments.

Uli, Andy and Julian
... for your always very, very critical comments about scientific work and your 'voluntary' participation as test subjects.

my parents
... for your backing all along my life, your support and everything you do for me.

Table of contents

Summary

The current study aimed to investigate basic mechanisms in the human brain involved in the development of fear and anxiety disorders. Therefore, a classical fear conditioning paradigm was applied to investigate the influence of cues and contexts. Two contexts were created in a virtual environment depicting similar office rooms connected by a corridor. In addition, screenshots were taken of each virtual scenario and controlled for entropy, brightness, valence, arousal and subjective complexity. These 48 pictures served as cues in the main experiment.

During two acquisition phases, participants were passively guided through the offices. Several aversive electric shocks (US) were administered in one room but not in the other. In this way, one room gradually became the anxiety context (CXT+), whereas the other room became the safety context (CXT-). Context conditioning was explicitly measured by skin conductance level while participants were guided through the virtual environments. Enhanced skin conductance was expected in CXT+ compared to CXT-. Furthermore, subjective ratings of the contexts were assessed in regard to valence, arousal and anxiety before, between and after conditioning.

Cue conditioning was assessed using electroencephalography (EEG). Event-related brain potentials (ERPs) were elicited by screenshots of the virtual environment depicting three different categories: the safety context (CXT-), the anxiety context at moments of US administration during conditioning (CXT+US), and the anxiety context at moments of no former US administration (CXT+noUS). Cue conditioning was expected in respect of increased ERP amplitudes evoked by CXT+US compared to CXT+noUS and CXT-. This enhanced ERP amplitudes were supposed to occur even in the absence of conscious awareness to the contingency of screenshot and US.

Results suggested contextual fear conditioning, as participants displayed increased skin conductance while traveling through CXT+ as compared to CXT-. This was further confirmed through subjective ratings, in which participants indicated a decreased valence and increased arousal and anxiety level for CXT+ as compared to CXT-. However, the investigation of ERP components P100, EPN and LPP revealed no significant differences in amplitudes between the cue categories CXT+US, CXT+noUS and CXT-. Moreover, no ERP evidence was found for contextual conditioning by comparing screenshots of CXT+ to CXT-.

    In conclusion, the current investigations demonstrated contextual anxiety using a virtual reality paradigm. However, cued fear conditioning can neither be confirmed nor falsified with the recent ERP measurements. This might be a consequence of the high complexity of the screenshots or perhaps an extinction of learning during the test phase, in which no USs were applied. Regardless, the current paradigm with highly controlled stimuli provides an outstanding possibility to investigate contextual conditioning and cues that are integrated into context. In the future, several methodological changes in regard to implicit measurements of brain activity are necessary to further understand anxiety evoked by contexts and fear evoked by cues and to transfer findings to the development of anxiety disorders.

Zusammenfassung

Ziel der vorliegenden Studie war die Untersuchung grundlegender Mechanismen im menschlichen Gehirn, die bei der Entstehung von Furcht und Angststörungen eine Rolle spielen.

In einem klassischen Furcht-Konditionierungsexperiment wurde der Einfluss von Auslösereizen (Cues) und von Kontexten untersucht. Dafür wurden zwei Kontexte in virtueller Realität (VR) gebaut, die ähnliche Büroräume darstellten und durch einen Flur miteinander verbunden waren. Zusätzlich wurden Screenshots der virtuellen Szenarien aufgenommen und hinsichtlich Entropie, Helligkeit, Valenz, Arousal und subjektiver Komplexität kontrolliert. Diese 48 Bilder dienten während des Experiments als Auslösereize.

In mehreren Konditionierungsphasen liefen die Versuchspersonen passiv auf vorher aufgenommenen Pfaden durch die Büros. In einem Raum wurden leicht schmerzhafte elektrische Reize (US) appliziert, im anderen nicht. Auf diese Weise veränderte sich ein Raum mit der Zeit zum Angst-Kontext (CXT+), während der andere Raum immer mehr zum Sicherheitskontext wurde (CXT-). Kontextkonditionierung wurde währenddessen explizit durch die Hautleitfähigkeit erfasst. Dabei war erhöhte Hautleitfähigkeit im CXT+ im Vergleich zum CXT- zu erwarten. Außerdem führten die Versuchsperson vor, während und nach der Konditionierung subjektive Bewertungen der Kontexte durch hinsichtlich der Valenz, ihrer Aufregung und ihrer Angst.

In der Test-Phase wurde Cue-Konditionierung mittels Elektroenzephalographie (EEG) untersucht. Screenshots des Sicherheitskontexts (CXT-), des Angst-Kontexts an Stellen, an denen zuvor ein elektrischer Reiz gegeben wurde, und des Angst-Kontexts an Orten in der VR, an denen vorher nie ein US kam. Die kurz präsentierten Bilder der Räume führten zu Spannungsänderungen im menschlichen Kortex, die als ereignis-korrelierte Potenziale (EKPs) analysiert wurden. Cue-Konditionierung wurde erwartet und sollte verifiziert werden durch erhöhte EKP Amplituden, die von CXT+US Stimuli evoziert wurden im Vergleich zu Amplituden, die CXT+noUS und CXT- hervorriefen. Die erhöhten Amplituden sollten sogar ohne Kontingenzbewusstsein der Versuchspersonen von Screenshot und US deutlich werden .

Die Ergebnisse zeigten eindeutige kontextuelle Furchtkonditionierung durch ein höheres Hautleitfähigkeitsniveau der Probanden im CXT+ als im CXT-. Zusätzlich bestätigten dies die subjektiven Ratings. Hier berichteten die Versuchspersonen eine niedrigere Valenz, höhere Aufregung und stärkere Angst im CXT+ als im CXT-. Untersucht man jedoch die EKP-Komponenten P100, EPN und LPP, finden sich keine signifikanten Amplitudenunterschiede ausgelöst durch die einzelnen Screenshotkategorien (CXT+US, CXT+noUS und CXT-). Außerdem wurden in der EKP-Analyse keine Hinweise auf die zuvor bestätigte Kontextkonditionierung gefunden.

Insgesamt zeigte die vorliegende Untersuchung induzierte Kontextangst evoziert durch das verwendete Paradigma in VR. Jedoch kann Cue-Konditionierung mit diesen EEG-Messungen weder bestätigt noch widerlegt werden. Dies könnte an der hohen Komplexität der Screenshots liegen oder an Extinktionlernen während der Test-Phase, in der keine USs appliziert wurden. Trotzdem beinhaltet das vorliegende Studiendesign mit den stark kontrollierten Stimuli die einzigartige Möglichkeit Kontext- und Cue-Konditionierung gleichzeitig zu untersuchen und zu vergleichen, wobei die Auslösereize in den Kontext integriert sind. Zukünftig sind einige Änderungen bezüglich der Methodik der EEG-Messung nötig, um weitere Aufschlüsse über die Entstehung von Angst, bezogen auf einen Kontext, und Furcht, ausgelöst durch einen expliziten Reiz, zu gewinnen und auf Angststörungen zu transferieren.

1 Introduction

1.1 Fear, anxiety and behavioral responses

The ability of appropriately coping with danger is indispensable for every living organism. Learning to recognize and avoid life-threatening situations and to respond adequately enhances survival. Hence, in the light of evolution fear and anxiety have developed as emotional strategies to help identifying risk and thereby influencing an animal's fitness essentially (Mineka & Öhman, 2002).

In 1970, R. C. Bolles studied reactions to danger and avoidance learning. He established the theory about *Species-Specific Defense Reactions* (SSDR). From this point of view, avoidance learning depends on the animal's innate defense system and on the kind of required defense reaction. If the response belongs to the innate defense system, the avoidance reaction will be acquired rapidly. In contrast, if the defense response is not part of the animal's innate system, the avoidance reaction will be slower. In the same way, learning of punishment contingencies even to a non-avoidance behavior can also lead to prevent specific actions (Bolles, 1970).

Fanselow (1994) described the defense behavior of rats elicited by threatening stimuli in his *predator imminence model*. According to this theory, three distinct defensive modes can be triggered depending on the animal's level of fear, which is influenced by the spatial distance of the threat and the temporal likelihood to get involved into a dangerous situation. *Pre-encounter defensive behavior* is elicited when the animal's level of fear is very low. This can be the case if a rat explores a certain area to find food while not perceiving a predator. The open space itself provides a potential danger, and thus, evokes this behavior. However, when a predator is detected by the rat, the fear level rises and the animal shows *post-encounter defensive behavior* including freezing or a potentiated startle response. The third mode of the system, the *circa-strike defensive behavior*, occurs when the animal is in direct contact with a predator evoking a superior level of fear. Distinctive animal reactions contain jumping, biting, audible vocalization, fight or flight. Fanselow (1994) also emphasized the animals' ability to switch between these imminence modes according to changes of the environmental threat.

Hitherto, many research studies use the startle reflex to investigate defensive behavior not only in rats but also in humans (Davis, Walker, Miles & Grillon, 2009;

Walker, Toufexis & Davis, 2003). In this aspect of behavioral analysis, it is necessary to differentiate between two primary defensive behavioral states: fear and anxiety. One can distinguish these states in terms of neural circuits and underlying molecular mechanisms of both emotions (Grillon, 2008).

Whether fear or rather anxiety is triggered depends heavily on the kind of eliciting stimulus (Grillon, 2008). Fear is evoked by imminent danger and clearly identifiable stimuli, which predict the threat, so called explicit cues. Phasic body reactions emerge such as increasing physiological arousal, alarm reaction, fight or flight, or decreasing the impact of threat, for example by reducing pain sensitivity (Blanchard, Yudko, Rodgers & Blanchard, 1993; Bolles & Fanselow, 1980; Carlsson et al., 2006; Grillon, 2008; Rhudy & Meagher, 2000). Additionally, fear narrows attention and inhibits competing responses (Grillon, 2008; Mowrer & Aiken, 1954; Vuilleumier, 2005). Anxiety, on the other hand, is a long-lasting emotional state, which is also known as 'sustained fear' (Grillon, 2008). It is elicited by a potentially dangerous context, which contains unpredictable threat. Particularly the inability to identify periods of safety evokes this chronic stress (Seligman, 1968; Seligman & Binik, 1977). In apprehension of potential danger, anxiety is characterized by an increased overall sensory sensitivity to threatening stimuli in a certain context (Baas, Nugent, Lissek, Pine & Grillon, 2004) and feelings of insecurity and helplessness (Grillon, 2002; Grillon, 2008).

Taking Fanselow's *predator imminence model*, the *pre-encounter defensive behavior* would be associated with anxiety, because animals are located in a potentially dangerous context, but no predator displaying a particular threatening cue is visible. Likewise, anxiety or sustained fear also occurs when danger is distal (*post-encounter*). In contrast, 'phasic fear' rises with the appearance of an explicit threatening stimulus like an approaching predator, so *circa-strike defensive behavior* is visible (Davis et al., 2009).

All in all, animal and human research emphasizes the importance to distinguish the distinct environmental stimuli in terms of cues or contexts, the particularly evoked emotion of fear or anxiety and the adequate behavioral responses.

1.2 Clinical insights

Anxiety disorder patients suffer from a dysfunction of perceiving and processing threatening stimuli or a malfunction in the behavioral or physiological response. Investigations of the prevalence of anxiety disorders in America revealed that 18% of the US population is affected by anxiety disorders (http://www.adaa.org/about-adaa/press-room/facts-statistics). Alonso et al. (2004) investigated the prevalence of anxiety disorders in six European countries and found that 13.6% of adults from Belgium, France, Germany, Italy, the Netherlands and Spain reported a life-time history of anxiety disorder. These numbers highlight the importance of research on understanding the mechanisms of fear and anxiety. According to DSM-IV criteria (American Psychiatric Association, 1994), anxiety disorders can be subdivided into seven categories: acute stress disorder, social phobia, generalized anxiety disorder (GAD), panic disorders, specific phobias, obsessive compulsive disorder and post-traumatic stress disorder (PTSD). Diagnostic evidence for general anxiety disorders is given by excessive anxiety and patients' worries that last for more than six month. Patients report difficulties in controlling their anxiety, which interferes with everyday life like work or social activities. Furthermore, symptoms like restlessness, fatigue, difficulty concentrating, irritability, muscle tension or sleep disturbance indicate anxiety disorder (DSM-IV, American Psychiatric Association, 1994).

Various dispositions in genetics, brain chemistry, personality and life events increase the risk of developing anxiety disorders (http://www.adaa.org/about-adaa/press-room/facts-statistics).

Altered processing of danger and safety signals is the most common explanation of the disease. Therefore, two mechanisms differ in patients and healthy controls during associations of a neutral and an aversive stimulus (Lissek et al., 2005). On the one hand, anxiety disorder patients show improved and faster associative learning between neutral and aversive stimulus (Orr & Roth, 2000). On the other hand, even when safety signals are presented, patients display increased fear reactions (Lissek et al., 2005). Specific phobias are directed to certain cues and classically associated with fear disorders like arachnophobia or aviophobia. In contrast, generalized anxiety goes along with anxiety disorders (Grillon, 2008). But some diseases like posttraumatic stress disorder (PTSD) are associated with both, discrete cues that elicit fear and certain contexts that increase the sustained anxiety and hypervigilance (American Psychiatric Association, 1994).

Although associative learning which links a certain threat stimulus with a coping strategy is absolutely necessary for life, mechanisms are still poorly understood. In order to help patients suffering from anxiety disorders, basic research is needed starting at the early stages of the development of the disease. Therefore, fear must be distinguished from anxiety and the emotion eliciting cues have to be investigated.

1.3   From classical conditioning to contextual fear conditioning

1.3.1   Classical conditioning

One simple form of associative learning is classical or Pavlovian conditioning. A lot of basic research is done in easily structured animals like snails or fruit flies using this paradigm. It gives a lot of information about brain mechanisms that are involved in the association between an originally neutral and a generally aversive stimulus (Aguilar, 2003).

In the classical conditioning paradigm an unconditioned stimulus (US, e.g. aversive electric shock or loud scream) is applied, which elicits an unconditioned response (UR, e.g. muscle contraction) without any necessity of former training. In a learning phase the unconditioned stimulus is timely and spatially paired with a neutral stimulus (e.g. tone or geometric figure). This temporal contiguity of unconditioned and neutral stimuli leads to an associative learning mechanism whereby the neutral becomes gradually the conditioned stimulus (CS). After conditioning, the CS elicits a similar behavioral and physiological reaction as the US, which is now termed as conditioned response (CR) (Pavlov, 1927).

In general, all mammals are capable of associating originally neutral objects or situations with danger or threat through Pavlovian conditioning due to its indispensability for survival (Mineka, 1979).

But also appetitive classical conditioning can occur in animals and humans. A classical paradigm of reward learning contains the proboscis extension response (PER) of honeybees (*apis mellifera*), which was recently standardized and described by Matsumoto, Menzel, Sandoz & Giurfa (2012). Here, bees learn the association between an odor (CS) and a reward of sugar solution (US). After several learning trials, bees extend their proboscis as a response to the odor alone, which displays the CR.

Requirements for associative learning are contiguity, contingency and predictability. The first, contiguity, implies that a temporal proximity between a CS and the US must be ensured to learn the associations (Rescorla, 1988). Second, contingency must be guaranteed, which refers to the information a present CS provides about an upcoming US in contrast to the absence of the CS. Furthermore, any expectation has to be evoked by the CS to be able to predict the US. All of the three aspects are involved in typical associative learning (Andreatta, 2010).

1.3.2 Fear conditioning

Fear conditioning basically describes the distinct learning to be afraid of a former neutral stimulus, which might predict threat and is therefore important for survival. In his preparedness theory, Seligman (1970) depicted that organisms are prepared to associate some events more likely with danger than others due to natural selection. Concerning phobias, Seligman's theory might especially be true for objects and situations that were dangerous to pre-technological man (Mineka & Öhman, 2002). In the light of evolution, phylogenetic relevant stimuli that were highly important for survival of our ancestors like dangerous predators, heights or open spaces are more likely to cause fears and phobias compared to contemporary ontogenetic threats like guns (Mineka & Öhman, 2002). To investigate this issue experimentally, pictures were presented displaying evolutionary relevant fear-objects like snakes or spiders and pictures showing contemporary relevant fear-objects like guns or knives. Results clearly indicate a more robust learning to the phylogenetic fear-relevant stimuli (Mineka & Öhman, 2002). In parallel, Mühlberger, Wiedemann, Herrmann & Pauli (2006) compared physiological reactions like for instance skin conductance level of spider-phobics and aviophobic patients by viewing pictures of spiders and flight accidents. Here, spider-phobic patients showed enhanced overall responsiveness to fear-relevant stimuli compared to aviophobic patients that only displayed increased physiological responses to flight-associated stimuli. The results confirmed the phylogenetic relevance of stimulus-associations that require an increased biological preparedness and therefore cause superior fear conditioning.

1.3.3 Contextual and cued fear conditioning

Not only single objects but also contexts are important for associative learning. Contextual representations can give a meaning to an event and even change the relevance of a situation, and therefore, have a huge impact on an animal's life. Maren, Phan & Liberzon (2013, p. 417) defined a context regarding to Spear (1973) very basically as *'the internal (cognitive and hormonal) and external (environmental and social) backdrop against which psychological processes operate.'*

Rudy, Huff & Matus-Amat (2004) transferred the classical conditioning paradigm to contextual and cued fear conditioning experiments with rodents. Thereby, an animal was placed into an experimental arena and received phasic auditory cues each paired with an electric shock to its feet. Contextual fear conditioning was revealed when the rodent was returned into the same experimental arena and showed freezing behavior. However, when the rodent sat in a different context but the auditory cue was presented, freezing behavior was triggered only by the cue. This is called auditory-cued fear conditioning (Blanchard & Blanchard, 1969).

When performing conditioning experiments, contextual representations are inevitable for associative learning. If a rat is foot shocked immediately or within a couple of seconds after being placed into a context, it shows almost no freezing behavior as indicator for fear in that context (Fanselow 1984, 1994; Rudy & O'Reilly, 1999). Consequently, it was concluded that the rat had not sufficiently explored the environment. So the brain could not build up any representation of the context, which could have been associated with the foot shock. However, if the rat was preexposed to the context, the immediate shock evoked fear response. Fanselow (1984, 1994) claimed it as a *context pre-exposure facilitation effect* (CPFE).

In animal as well as in human research, conditioned stimuli can either be composed of explicit cues or of contextual stimuli. When the threat is predicted by explicit cues like a tone or a flashing light (Grillon & Davis, 1997), cued fear conditioning takes place. Fear arises in the participants for a distinct period of time whenever threat signals precisely announce upcoming danger. Hence, cue conditioning is a model for phasic fear (Craske et al., 2009; Davis et al., 2009; Grillon, 2008).

In contrast, if there is no explicit predictor for an US, conditioning to a context occurs. Contexts provide animals with information about a particular odor, floor texture, sound level, illumination, shape and size (Rudy, 2004). So, context conditioning evokes anxiety, due to the unpredictability of the aversive stimulus, and leads to hypervigilance and persistent signs of distress (Grillon, 2002). Therefore, context conditioning is a model for sustained fear or anxiety (Craske et al., 2009; Davis et al., 2010; Grillon, 2008). The sensibility of animals and humans to classical fear conditioning is depicted in several studies. Fanselow (1990) investigated one-trial contextual conditioning in a rat experiment. Even when the rat was placed for the second time in the anxiety context where it had previously perceived an aversive stimulus, the association between the particular context and threat was strong enough to evoke freezing behavior. But in principal, also humans are very sensitive to conditioning, since several studies (Bröckelmann et al., 2011; Steinberg et al., 2011) showed associative learning in humans despite just a unique contiguous CS and US presentation (one trial learning). However, especially in human research it remains under debate how far associative learning is implemented by cue conditioning or exclusively triggered by the whole context.

1.4   Neural correlates of fear, anxiety and conditioning

For many years, neural correlates of classical and contextual fear conditioning have been investigated in animals as well as in humans. On a neurobiological level of research, a differentiation of neural systems between fear and anxiety is suggested. Thereby, fear is a phasic and short duration aversive state whereas anxiety depicts a sustained and long lasting aversive state. These states are subjected to distinct neural substrates, which elicit appropriate defensive responses (Grillon, 2002; Grillon, 2008).

Bechara et al. (1995) performed experiments studying subjects' automatic reactions to a conditioned dangerous signal and their explicit knowledge about the stimulus contingencies in patients with certain brain lesions. The results showed a clear dissociation between the implicit/non-declarative and the explicit/declarative learning. A patient with bilateral amygdala damage was unable to acquire conditioned automatic responses, whereas a patient with bilateral hippocampus damage did not acquire declarative facts. A patient with lesions of both the amygdala and the hippocampus revealed impairment in explicit and implicit learning.

Studies on the brain of rodents showed that threat is highly processed in the amygdala (Roozendaal, McEwen & Chattarji, 2009). Information is sent from the basolateral nuclei (BLA) to the central nucleus of the amygdala (CeA) or to the Bed Nucleus of Stria Terminalis (BNST), respectively (Walker et al., 2003). Both brain structures, CeA and BNST, are highly connected and even consist of similar cell morphology (Alheid et al., 1998). Nevertheless, the central amygdala is crucial for the response to discrete threatening cues (phasic fear) (Alvarez, Biggs, Chen, Pine & Grillon, 2008; LeDoux, 2000), whereas the BNST mediates anxiety responses to chronic stress induced by a context of temporally uncertain danger (sustained fear) (Alvarez, Chen, Bodurka, Kaplan & Grillon, 2011; Davis et al., 2009; Grillon, 2008; Walker et al., 2003). Additionally, many studies point out (Alvarez et al., 2008; Hasler et al., 2007; Marschner, Kalisch, Vervliet, Vansteenwegen & Büchel, 2008) that also the hippocampus is crucially involved in context conditioning and sustained anxiety. All these aspects demonstrate that a well functioning brain network, specialized in processing cued fear stimuli or contextual anxiety stimuli, is necessary for an appropriate response to any environmental danger.

According to cue and contextual fear conditioning, neural representations must be analyzed more precisely, even according to the stimuli, which consolidate conditioning. Rudy et al. (2004) described a *dual representation model* of a context. In this view, contexts can be represented in two different ways in the brain: the *features view* and the *conjunctive view*. Classical fear conditioning can lead to an increased association between one distinct and another stimulus represented by a feature and/or between one distinct and another conjunctive represented stimulus. If the environment is perceived as a variety of independent elements and single features, the neocortical system is involved in processing these particular cues. On the other hand, if features are processed in its entirety and perceived as a new unitary representation, the conjunction is processed by neural interactions of cortical structures and subcortical areas like hippocampus and amygdala.

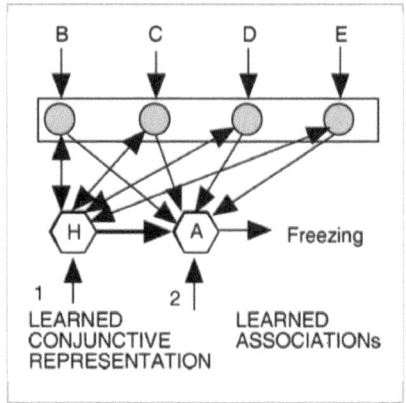

Figure 1: A model of the two-process theory of classical fear conditioning by Rudy et al. (2004). B, C, D and E represent sensory threat cues that are processed in the neocortex. If stimuli are processed in a feature representation, neuronal information will be transferred directly to the amygdala, which elicits fear response e.g. freezing. However, if stimuli are processed in a conjunctive representation, neuronal information will be transmitted to the hippocampus and then to the amygdala, which elicits fear response.

To go one step further, Rudy et al. (2004) postulated a *two-process theory* of classical fear conditioning. In this model, conditioning can either occur by linking the hippocampal-dependent conjunctive representations to the amygdala or by connecting the feature representation to the amygdala (Fig. 1).

First, independently processed features are bound into one unitary representation by the hippocampus (Wicklegren, 1979) that rapidly and automatically stores conjunctive representations just as an organism is attending to its environment (O'Reilly & Rudy, 2001). Moreover, the hippocampus supports declarative memory consolidation (O'Reilly & Rudy, 2001) and is connected via its ventral part to the amygdala. During contextual fear conditioning, the hippocampus must bind the features into a conjunctive representation and as a consequence of US delivering, associative connections between the hippocampus and the amygdala are strengthened. The input pattern of features is stored as a conjunctive representation, so the presentation of a subset of these features will activate the memory for an entire input pattern. This mechanism is crucial for memory retrieval as well as for responding and acting to environmental stimuli (Squire, 1992).

The second mechanism of Rudy's *two-process theory* involves the BLA that supports the cue-shock-association. On the one hand, the amygdala perceives input from the conjunctive representation of the hippocampus, on the other hand, cortical representations of features directly innervate the BLA. In turn, the CeA evokes conditioned freezing responses in rats.

This model points out that fear conditioning to single features is not necessarily mediated by the hippocampus but it requires the strengthening of associative connections between features and the amygdala. However, the hippocampus is essentially involved in building the conjunctive representation of a context. In summary, the *dual representation model* suggests the establishment of contextual fear conditioning either with single environmental features or with the conjunctive contextual representation.

1.5 Physiology

'Emotions are action dispositions' (Lang, 1995, p. 372). Generally described by Lang (1995), the basis for feeling emotions provide an appetitive motivational system and a defense motivational system. Importantly, the latter contains fear and anxiety. It elicits avoidance and escape behavior and is therefore characterized by protection and withdrawing. Reactions to threatening stimuli are also assigned to this kind of motivational system. According to Lang (1995), indices of affective responses regarding anxiety are described in three reactive systems: first, on an explicit level by subjectively judging and evaluating the emotional state in this case for instance a high score of arousal; second, on a behavioral level by reacting in a certain behavioral sequence-pattern of avoidance or flight; third on a physiological level mediated by somatic and autonomic systems. In this study, fear reactions are also recorded via physiological changes in terms of an altered skin conductance level and different amplitudes in brain potentials by processing stimuli associated with either safety or danger.

1.5.1 Electrodermal activity (EDA)

Electrodermal activity is a commonly used physiological measurement to monitor body responses to distinct stimulation (Lang, 1995). Therefore, skin conductance level (SCL) was recorded. Lykken & Venables (1971) described that skin conductance depends on three aspects: first, the density of sweat glands that are located in the chosen skin region; second, the degree of 'psycho-activity' of the sweat glands in this area; and third, the size of skin area that is in contact with the electrolyte which is used to improve conductance. As sweat gland density and 'psych-activity' are highest on the foot and the palms (Kappeler-Setz, Gravenhorst, Schumm, Arnich & Tröster, 2013), while the latter is easier accessible in human studies, this region is ordinarily used for psychological research (Günther et al., 2013). The here recorded tonic skin conductance refers to the skin conductance level during a specific time period, whereas skin conductance response (SCR) refers to phasic activity evoked by discrete stimuli.

Many recent conditioning experiments used this method and reported a greater SCR to stimuli that were associated with danger or fear compared to stimuli predicting safety (Baas, van Ooijen, Goudriaan & Kenemans, 2008; Huff, Zielinski, Fecteau, Brady & LaBar, 2010; Marschner et al., 2008). From an evolutionary perspective, such fear stimulation excites the human sympathetic nerve system, which leads to an increased activation of the sweat glands. This mechanism prepares the body for an adequate response and provides a faster reaction time in dangerous situations (Fenz & Eppstein, 1967; Lang, Davis & Öhman, 2000; Öhman, 2009; Öhman & Soares, 1994).

1.5.2 Electroencephalography (EEG)

Already in the beginning of the 20th century, Hans Berger (1929) pioneered the research on cortical brain areas using electroencephalography. The human cortex consists of six cell layers, which are formed by different types of neurons. The most important part concerning EEG recordings is layer five, because it contains the cell bodies of pyramidal cells. These cells are very large and, in contrast to other neurons, the only cells which project into further cell layers. When an action potential arrives at one of these neurons, a very small electric field is generated. In case of thousands of cells firing at the same time, the amplified signal is large enough to be recorded in terms of one end of the developing dipole on the scalp surface. The more neurons fire regularly, the stronger is the signal, the higher is the amplitude and the lower is the frequency. The main advantage of this method displays the high time resolution, whereas a disadvantage reveals the poor spatial resolution of the whole brain because potentials can only be recorded from the scalp and give poor information about involved subcortical brain areas (Bear, Connors & Paradiso, 2007).

Characteristic event-related brain potentials arise, depending on the kind of stimulus, its physical properties, riveted attention and emotional relevance for the participant. Event-related potentials (ERPs) are defined as '*small changes in the electrical activity of the brain that are recorded from the scalp and that are brought about by some external or internal event.*' (Coles & Rugg, 1995 in Handy, 2005). For instance, a visual or auditory stimulus can evoke a distinct pattern of potential changes in particular areas of the cortex. Relative amplitudes and latencies of certain components can give a clue about the neuronal resources that are needed to process specific stimulation.

Many studies associated the P100, which occurs as a positive peak about 100 ms after stimulus onset and is recorded from posterior scalp electrodes, with attention (Luck, Woodman & Vogel, 2000). Pioneering experiments found higher ERP amplitudes of attended stimuli compared to unattended stimuli between 60 and 100 ms after stimulus onset (Hillyard & Münte, 1984). Their results suggested that attention modulates stimulus processing latest in this time interval. Hillyard, Vogel & Luck (1998) described a sensory 'gain control' mechanism, which can be visualized in a larger P100 ERP component elicited by an attended-location stimulus relative to an ignored-location stimulus.

Additionally, early selective attention also modulates ERPs around 150 ms as Junghöfer, Bradley, Elbert & Lang (2001) demonstrated. Here, participants viewed pictures of emotional scenes while EEG was recorded. It could be shown that high arousing pictures elicited a more relative negative potential around 150 ms stimulus onset compared to low arousing pictures and neutral pictures. Moreover, when considering early event-related potentials evoked by visual stimuli, picture properties have to be taken into account. Bradley, Hamby, Löw & Lang (2007) investigated the influence of physical picture properties like brightness, contrast and spatial frequency on the ERPs. They found the largest effects of picture composition in a time window between 150 and 250 ms after stimulus onset.

Another relevant ERP component is the early posterior negativity (EPN), which occurs 240-280 ms after stimulus-onset over occipital and parietal areas of the scalp (Mühlberger et al., 2008; Wieser, Pauli, Reicherts & Mühlberger, 2010). This amplitude can also be affected by picture properties. Bradley et al. (2007) showed less positivity to figure-ground pictures compared to scenes over occipital sensors. In general, the EPN is a positive potential, which shows relatively less positivity to affective pictures, pleasant or unpleasant, compared to neutral pictures (Schupp, Junghöfer, Weike & Hamm, 2004). For that reason, the component's name contains 'negativity' though it is an overall positive change of brain potential, but decreasing negative parts are relevant (Schupp et al., 2004).

Furthermore, an ERP occurring in a time window of 400-800 ms after stimulus-onset is the late positive potential (LPP). Schupp et al. (2000) revealed that this centro-parietal emerging potential is modulated by motivational relevance. They compared the processing of emotional relevant pictures to neutral ones and showed an enhanced late positive shift especially when caused by affective and arousing stimuli. Here it was concluded that the LPP displays an intrinsic reflection of emotional processing and examines facilitated attention to emotional stimuli (Cuthbert, Schupp, Bradley, Birbaumer & Lang, 2000). Bradley et al. (2007) showed that this effect is even independent of the physical stimulus properties consisting of figure-ground contrasts or scenes. These results are highly important for conditioning experiments due to the fact that according to previously mentioned experiments conditioned stimuli contain increased emotional relevance and higher arousing, and therefore, should elicit higher LPP amplitude.

In David Meyer-Heintze's diploma thesis (2011), conditioning effects were recorded via event-related brain potentials. Hereby, the analysis was focused on three distinct ERP components described above, in particular P100, early posterior negativity (EPN) and late positive potential (LPP). At first, a fear conditioning paradigm was applied in a virtual environment containing two office rooms, one with red and the other with green carpet. Participants were guided through these offices and perceived conditioning in terms of administered shocks in one of the rooms but not in the other.

So, an anxiety and a safety context were created. For measuring ERPs relying on the context and cue conditioning in the test phase, screenshots of the virtual office rooms were presented depicting the safety context (CXT-) or depicting the anxiety context at a moment when a US was administered (CXT+US) or when no US was presented (CXT+noUS). Results depicted a more negative EPN potential for screenshots of CXT+US compared to pictures of CXT+noUS and CXT-. This indicates not only contextual fear conditioning to the anxiety context but also a more precisely cue conditioning to pictures displaying CXT+US compared to CXT+noUS even without participants' contingency awareness. However, further analysis revealed that this cue conditioning effect is only true when the office room with the red carpet was used as CXT+. Furthermore, stimuli were not controlled for picture properties like brightness and complexity.

The recent study exactly aimed to investigate whether the effects shown in the Meyer-Heintze's diploma thesis (2011) indeed arose due to contextual and cue conditioning or due to stimulus properties like carpet color or picture composition. Therefore, in the beginning of this work, highly controlled stimulus material was created in terms of similar office rooms and stimulus pictures with the same properties and the same ERP components were investigated.

1.6 Fear conditioning in virtual reality

When designing a scientific experiment, it is always a challenge to increase the ecological validity as far as possible while still maintaining the experimental control. Therefore, virtual reality (VR) turned out to be a great research tool because participants reported a high feeling of presence of actually being in the displayed environment. Even distinct experimental conditions can be changed very easily (Bohil, Alicea & Biocca, 2011). Today, virtual realities are established and frequently used in exposure therapy (e.g. Maltby, Kirsch, Mayers & Allen, 2002; Viaud-Delmon, Warusfel, Seguelas, Rio & Jouvent, 2006) and pain remediation for example in burn victims (Hoffmann et al., 2006).

Freire, De Carvalho, Joffily, Zin & Nardi (2010) investigated whether a virtual scenario of bus driving induces anxiety in patients suffering from panic disorder with agoraphobia. On a physiological level, patients showed higher skin conductance level, respiratory rate and tidal volume. These data suggested that this technology could be used to control experimental conditions and at the same time to precisely determine how patients respond to virtual contexts and specific cues, which are very similar to real life situations.

For that reason, the recent study also uses the virtual reality technology for classical fear conditioning. The paradigm is based on the diploma thesis written by David Meyer-Heintze (2011) containing a pre-acquisition, acquisition and test phase. Here, two modified office rooms served as virtual contexts connected via a corridor. Using virtual realities, independent variables could be determined easily before the main experiment whilst dependent variables like skin conductance level and subjective ratings were recorded in the course of the experimental procedure. During the acquisition phase of the experiment participants were guided several times through virtual contexts and perceived moderate painful electric stimuli in one (anxiety context, CXT+) but not in the other context (safety context, CXT-). In the acquisition phase as well as in the test phase, stimuli were presented on a powerwall in order to further increase stimulus validity.

1.7   Hypotheses and goals of the recent experiment

Aim of the research was the investigation of not only contextual fear associations in a fear conditioning paradigm, but also the demonstration of cued fear in the same experimental design. This should give information about the development of fear and anxiety and about the understanding of associated disorders. The main goal of this master thesis was to enlighten the neural cortical representations of contextual and cue information during fear conditioning. Therefore, the fear conditioning paradigm used in David Meyer-Heintze's diploma thesis (2011) was used in order to replicate and validate his findings with better controlled stimuli.

In this paradigm, fear conditioning was conducted in virtual reality. In the acquisition phase, participants were guided through two virtual office rooms connected via a corridor. Since in one room unconditioned stimuli in terms of electric shocks were administered, this room became gradually the anxiety context (CXT+), whereas the other room, in which no US was applied, became the safety context (CXT-). The following test phase should resolve contextual and cue conditioning. Hence, screenshots of the two office contexts were presented in three categories. They either depicted the safety context (CXT-), or showed the anxiety context at a moment of US presentation (CXT+US) or the anxiety context at a moment of no US administration (CXT+noUS).

A paradigm was used which provided information about the processing of the context as a whole or single features in a context, when participants underwent aversive conditioning. Physiological reactions promised to give some indication about responses to the whole context or even more detailed processing of single features of the context. In the recent study, screenshots of the anxiety context, at a moment when an electric shock was presented, should also be more relevant to the subjects and should therefore evoke a stronger early posterior negativity.

Dependent variables were subjective ratings of valence, arousal and anxiety before, between and after conditioning as indicators for contextual conditioning. In parallel, skin conductance levels were recorded during pre-acquisition and acquisition as a physiological measurement for contextual fear conditioning. Furthermore, in the test-phase physiological parameters were recorded via event-related brain potentials (P100, EPN, LPP) to resolve contextual and cue conditioning.
The following hypotheses were tested:

1. Contextual fear conditioning was expected.

    a. Participants were explicitly asked for the associative learning between the anxiety context (CXT+) and the electric shock (US) after conditioning. Aware participants were expected to rate context-US contingency correctly.

    b. Moreover, on a subjective level, verbal ratings of valence, arousal and anxiety were assessed after pre-acquisition, during acquisition and after conditioning. We hypothesized similar ratings after pre-acquisition, but lower valence and higher arousal and anxiety levels in the conditioned context.

    c. The physiological response could be analyzed by comparing the skin conductance levels in the conditioning phase when participants were passively guided through the anxiety (CXT+) and the safety (CXT-) context. Hereby, we expected increased SCL in the CXT+ compared to the CXT-.

2. Furthermore, it was also hypothesized that cue conditioning took place. This should be visible in higher amplitudes of electro-cortical responses to screenshots displaying the anxiety context at a moment of US presentation (CXT+US) compared to stimuli of the danger context without US presentation (CXT+noUS) and pictures of the safety context (CXT-). Particularly, the EPN component in which evidence for cue conditioning was already shown (Meyer-Heintze, 2011) should reveal an increased relative negativity for CXT+US stimuli compared to CXT+noUS and CXT-.

3. This effect should arise even without the subjects' explicit contingency awareness between US and screenshots depicting the time point of US administration (CXT+US).

2 Methods

2.1 Preparation of the experiment – pilot study

As mentioned above, the paradigm of the diploma thesis by David Meyer-Heintze (2011) showed promising results in terms of monitoring the differentiation between contextual and cue conditioning in virtual reality with electroencephalographic recordings. Due to the fact that the presented stimuli were poorly controlled, further investigations were necessary.

Moreover, in particular early event-related brain potentials (ERPs) beginning around 150 ms are highly sensitive to the properties of the eliciting stimulus (Bradley et al., 2007), so more experiments were needed comprising controlled stimulus material. For all these reasons, a pilot study was performed to create two easily distinguishable office rooms in virtual reality that evoked equal subjective levels of pleasantness, arousal and complexity. Furthermore, for the EEG test-phase, new screenshots had to be taken and carefully chosen. Selection was done aiming for similar physical properties like brightness and entropy level. Additionally, they were supposed to subjectively appear equal in terms of pleasantness, arousal and complexity (Wessa et al., 2010).

2.1.1 New stimulus material

2.1.1.1 Rebuilding the virtual environment

In the pre-study the two existing office rooms applied in Meyer-Heintze's diploma thesis (2011) and further studies (e.g. Glotzbach-Schoon et al., 2013) were adapted using the *Hammer Editor* of the *Source Engine* from the *Valve Corporation* (Bellevue, USA). This software is mainly used in computer games like Half-Life 2, but served here as medium to adjust the original virtual environments in shape, furniture, carpet colors, view out of the windows and pictures on the walls.

The two offices were changed into quadratic shape and were connected by an elongated corridor. Since the comparability of the two rooms was essential for the main experiment, each office had to contain similar equipment and the same amount of furniture. A detailed list is shown in the supplement (A).

In the diploma thesis (Meyer-Heintze, 2011), ERP-data reached significance just for the EPN component and that only in the office room with red compared to the room with green carpet. This color effects might be a priming mechanisms as red represents danger and green signifies safety in many everyday experiences. Literature discusses controversially if red induces avoidance motivation because it signals an upcoming danger (Mehta & Zhu, 2009) or it enhances approach behavior. From a biological point of view, red lips testify an attractive and healthy partner with high receptiveness (Elliot & Niesta, 2008). All in all, many studies showed that the color red influences human behavior (Elliot, Maier, Binser, Friedman & Pekrun, 2009). Moreover, Schupp, Junghöfer, Weike & Hamm (2003) found an explicitly increased EPN to evolutionary relevant pictures compared to neutral pictures. For this reason, the new color of the carpet in the two office rooms was chosen carefully. The original red carpet was modified in *Adobe Photoshop CS4* (version 11.0; Adobe Systems GmbH, Munich) by extending the shades of red ten steps into blue direction and ten steps into yellow direction. So two new shades of red color, a blue-red and a brown-red, were created and assigned into one of the rooms each (Fig. 2).

The view out of the window was also a prominent feature of the original virtual environment. One office room seemed to be built in a big city with skyscrapers visible in the windows. In contrast, the view out of the window of the second office revealed a hilly landscape with few one family houses. On the one hand, these different scenarios very much characterized the environments and helped the subjects to distinguish between the two rooms. But on the other hand, the differing views out of two rooms that are placed in the exact same building, appeared strange and artificial. Therefore, the newly created virtual space was set into a city. Looking out of the window, participants could now observe a similar environment from different perspectives without any distinct buildings or scenarios.

Lastly, eye-catching features in a context are pictures on the walls, which in this case occupied a very prominent space and also attracted the participants' attention. In the pilot study, the five wall pictures in each room were selected from neutral IAPS pictures (International Affective Picture System; pictures number 1121, 5390, 5395, 7160, 7247, 7248, 7249, 7547, 7820, 7830; Lang, Bradley & Cuthbert, 1999) according to a medium valence and arousal level and then equally distributed into the rooms (valence: $t(4)$ = -1.463, p = .217; arousal: $t(4)$ = .462, p = .668). All these modifications of the virtual environment should improve the comparability of the stimulus material in the main experiment.

Furthermore, in the pilot study paths were recorded through each office room, starting in the corridor. They lasted for 110 s in one and 111 s in the other room, respectively, and ended again in the corridor. Figure 2 depicts the two new office rooms right after entering one room.

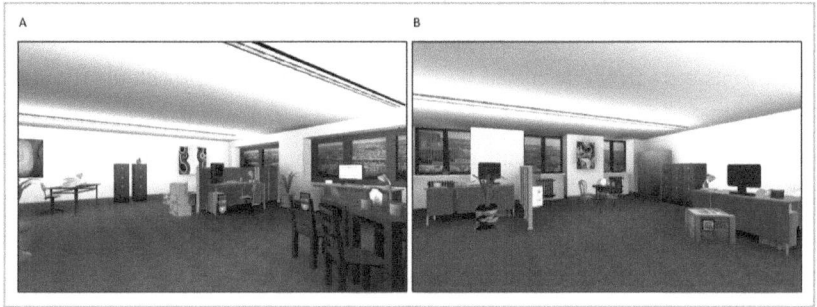

Figure 2: The two newly created office rooms. 2A depicts the room with brown-red carpet and 2B represents the room with blue-red carpet.

2.1.1.2 New screenshots

As a next step, screenshots were taken of the virtual environment from which pictures could be selected serving as stimuli in the test-phase. These pictures of the office contexts were presented in the main experiment to evoke event-related brain potentials. For that reason, starting the pre-recorded path through the offices, screenshots of the virtual rooms were taken every 2 seconds. Excluding pictures of the corridor, 42 potential stimuli in each room were created for the EEG experiment. To control for physical properties, entropy levels were calculated in *MATLAB* (version 7.11.1, MathWorks, USA). The mean entropy values of all 42 screenshots did not differ between the two rooms, $t(41)$ = .477, p = .636. Moreover, RGB-values comparing the brightness of the pictures of both rooms were determined applying *Adobe Photoshop CS4* (version

11.0, Munich, Germany). It could be shown that the created stimuli of the two rooms did not differ in brightness, $t(41) = -1.357, p = .182$.

2.1.2   Evaluation of the stimulus material

2.1.2.1   Sample and procedure

In order to investigate the subjective perception of the screenshots, 14 participants (8 females; mean age: 24.7; $SD = 3.97$) took part in the pilot study. They observed the virtual environment on the powerwall using *Cybersession* software (version 5.3.38). Participants were passively guided via the pre-recorded paths through the two newly created office rooms. After that, subjects were asked to rate which office seemed more pleasant. Additionally, participants saw each screenshot and were asked to rate their subjective feelings of valence, arousal and picture complexity directly after observing each picture individually. The rating experiment was created with *Presentation* software (version 15.1, Neurobehavioral Systems, Inc.).

2.1.2.2   Results and conclusions

Results showed that seven subjects preferred the room with the red-brown carpet color (Fig. 2A) and six the other office with red-blue (Fig. 2B), one participant could not decide, so he rated both rooms equally pleasant. Comparing these results, χ^2-test revealed that the overall valence of both offices was on the same level, $\chi^2(1) = .076, p = .783$.

Data suggest that for the conditioning procedure, the newly created virtual contexts did not differ before conditioning. Therefore, any significant effect during conditioning could be ascribed to the experimental manipulation instead of virtual reality effects. Besides, screenshot ratings of both offices neither differed in valence, $t(41) = 1.704; p = .096$, nor in arousal, $t(41) = -.384; p = .703$, and picture complexity, $t(41) = -.278; p = .783$.

Now, the most suitable screenshots of each office room were chosen for the experiment that showed similar physical picture properties and comparable subjective ratings of valence, arousal and complexity. Therefore, 24 out of 42 stimuli per room were selected and analyzed concerning all described parameters. Mean values and t-test statistics are depicted in Table 1 and clarify that the screenshots of both rooms do not differ significantly in the listed objective and subjective properties. Room 1 refers to the office with brown-red carpet and room 2 to the office with blue-red carpet.

Table 1: Objective and subjective picture properties of the 24 selected screenshots of each office room, mean values (*M*), standard deviation (*SD*) and t-tests.

	room 1		room 2		statistics	
	M	*SD*	*M*	*SD*	*T*	*p*
entropy	70972.33	4225.47	70083.83	2542.32	0.877	n.s.
RGB-value	154.70	7.12	157.96	6.78	-1.50	n.s.
valence	5.30	0.53	5.25	0.47	0.315	n.s.
arousal	4.65	0.29	4.68	0.28	-0.447	n.s.
complexity	5.85	0.97	5.79	0.88	0.261	n.s.

t-tests: $p > .05$: not significant (n.s.)

Furthermore, the 24 pictures were divided into two groups, which were presented during the experiment with or without US, respectively. Focus lay on the time interval, which was at least 4 s between two consecutive stimuli of different conditions in one room. In total eight experimental procedures were designed to pseudo-randomize the order of the two rooms in the acquisition phase, the anxiety (CXT+) and the safety context (CXT-) and the screenshot group which was associated either with (CXT+US) or without US (CXT+noUS) in the anxiety context.

In sum, the screenshots that were investigated in the pilot study should now be well adapted for the main study.

2.2   Sample

Participants were recruited via the local online platform *wuewowas.de*. At first a pre-screening by phone was conducted to exclude psychology students and people with excessive alcohol or illegal drug consume, regular intake of centrally active medication, severe illnesses or psychological disorders, poor eyesight, color blindness, left-handedness and pre-experience in similar conditioning experiments in virtual reality (supplement C).

In total 32 subjects took part in the experiment. Four unaware participants were excluded from further data evaluation because they obviously were not able to explicitly recall the CXT+US contingency. Therefore 28 subjects (13 females) aged between 18 and 33 (M = 23.81, SD = 3.98) were included in data analysis.

Participants were invited to the powerwall laboratory where they perceived a detailed written explanation about the experimental procedure. The study was approved by the Ethics Committee of the Medical Faculty of the University of Würzburg. The experiment lasted about two hours and was generally refunded with 16 Euros.

2.3 Material

2.3.1 Stimulus material

2.3.1.1 Aversive electric stimulation

In order to elicit fear, a mildly painful electric stimulus served as an unconditioned stimulus (US) in the experiment, administered by a *Digitimer Constant Current Stimulator Model DS7A* (Digitimer Ltd, Hertfordshire, England). The US consisted of a 50 Hz pulse, which lasted 200 ms (Andreatta, Mühlberger, Yarali, Gerber & Pauli, 2010). Before the pre-acquisition phase started, each subject's individual pain threshold was determined. Therefore, the electrode was placed at the participants' right inner forearm. Several electric stimuli were administered. Subjects rated their feeling of pain on a scale from 0 (*no sensation at all*) until 10 (*unbearable pain*) directly after each shock. Especially highlighted was score 4, because this estimation should be chosen when the stimulus elicited *just perceptible pain*. The current of the electric stimuli was increased in 0.5 mA steps, starting with 0 mA, until the participant rated a stimulus on the scale above 4. Then a descending series of electric stimuli was initiated, also in 0.5 mA steps until the subject scored the electric stimulus below 4. This procedure was repeated twice. Then, the individual stimulus intensity was calculated by averaging the four current intensities that were rated by at least 4. This intensity was increased by 30% to assure an aversive, moderate pain feeling for the subjects and to avoid habituation. This stimulus was administered to the participant and once again rated on the 10-point pain scale. The shock was regarded as well adapted, when the score was above 4 and the subject affirmed his or her agreement to deal with the pain in the experiment. Moreover, valence and arousal ratings of the electric stimulus were requested. The valence scale ranged from 0 (*extremely negative*) to 100 (*extremely positive*) and the arousal scale from 0 (*not arousing at all*) to 100 (*extremely arousing*) (supplement G).

2.3.1.2 Screenshots in test-phase

In the test-phase of the experiment, screenshots depicting the virtual office rooms were shown for 1000 ms to evoke event-related potentials in the cortex of the brain. Inter-stimulus intervals varied between 1500 and 2500 ms. The screenshots were carefully chosen according to their physical properties and subjective ratings developed in the pilot study mentioned above. Depending on the experimental condition, 24 screenshots of the safety context (CXT-) and 24 of the anxiety context (12 CXT+US; 12 CXT+noUS) were presented three times, so the EEG experiment comprised a total number of 144 trials. As already explained above, safety and anxiety contexts as well as groups of screenshots with and without electric shock were counterbalanced across participants.

2.3.2 Data acquisition

2.3.2.1 Subjective data

Data about the subjects' personal mood and emotional state were collected using standardized questionnaires at the beginning of the study and ratings integrated into the experimental procedure.

2.3.2.1.1 Questionnaires

Before starting the conditioning experiment, participants were provided with questionnaires, which were rendered anonymously. In general, questionnaires are a good option for investigating not only the subject's demographic data, but also very subjective feelings, as e.g. Jackson, Payne, Nadel & Jacobs (2005) showed, that stress modulates classical fear conditioning.

First, demographic information (age, gender, education, profession and handedness) was collected. Moreover, inclusion criteria were requested another time in written form, especially in regard to the subject's liability to nausea (supplement F). This is an inevitable aspect to control in virtual environment studies because susceptible people often reported a feeling of sickness when moving through virtual reality (Bohil et al., 2011).

The Positive and Negative Affect Schedule (PANAS; Watson, Clark & Tellegen, 1988; German version by Krohne, Egloff, Kohlmann & Tausch, 1996) determines the subject's momentarily emotional state in dominant two dimensions. The positive affect part describes the extent of a person's enthusiasm, activity, attention, lethargy and sadness, whereas the negative affect part gathers the degree of negative tension, petulance, nervousness and anxiety. The questionnaire consists of two mood scales containing ten items each, to investigate positive and negative affect.

Moreover, the subjects' fear of fear was investigated by the anxiety sensitivity index (ASI; Reiss, Peterson, Gursky & McNally, 1986; German version by Alpers & Pauli, 2001). In this questionnaire, authors examined anxiety sensitivity and focused negative implications that were associated with anxiety experiences. Here, 16 items request the subjects' anxiety. It can be answered in a five-point scale depending on the participant's own estimations.

The Behavioral Inhibition System and Behavioral Approach System questionnaire (BIS/BAS; Carver & White, 1994; German version by Strobel, Beauducel, Debener & Brocke, 2001) is constructed in 24 items, which can be rated by the subjects on a four-point scale. The questionnaire gives indications of the subject's sensitivity to reward and punishment. Therefore, the BIS is responsive for cues of punishment and a measure of vulnerability to anxiety. The BAS, in contrast, is sensitive to cues of reward including the investigation of a subject's fun seeking and drive.

Finally, the State-Trait-Anxiety-Inventory (Spielberger, Gorsuch & Lushene, 1970; German version by Laux, Glanzmann, Schaffner & Spielberger, 1981) examined the participants' current and general anxiety. This questionnaire differentiated anxiety in two kinds. First, anxiety is seen as an emotional state, which is characterized by tension, apprehensiveness, nervousness and increased activity of the autonomic nerve system.

Second, trait anxiety is investigated which refers to subjects' estimations of a situation as threatening. Stable inter-individual differences become evident in a way that high anxious individuals tend to classify more situations as dangerous compared to subjects with low trait anxiety. The STAI-state as well as the STAI-trait part each consists of 20 items. In both parts, participants were asked to rate on a four-point scale.

2.3.2.1.2   Explicit ratings: Valence, arousal, anxiety, US-expectancy, US-contingency and screenshot affiliation

The experiment consisted of several phases in which subjective ratings were used as dependent variable. Levels of the participants' valence, arousal and anxiety were asked three times during the conditioning: directly after pre-acquisition, after acquisition phase 1 and after acquisition phase 2 (see Fig. 3). Objective of these ratings was not only the investigation of the participant's feeling but also the monitoring of gradual changes of their feelings during the conditioning paradigm. Rating was conducted in the following way: An instruction slide was shown on the powerwall that described the procedure and the actions that were required of the participant. Afterwards, a screenshot serving as a reminder of the context depicting the entrance of one of the office rooms was shown. Meanwhile, a question popped up concerning the feeling when the subject was guided through the depicted room, requesting valence, arousal or anxiety estimations respectively. Answers could be given on a scale from 0 to 100. In the valence rating, 0 meant a *very negative feeling*, 100 implied a *very positive feeling* in the distinct office room. The range of the arousal rating also was from 0, *not arousing at all*, until 100, *extremely arousing*. Anxiety levels could be scaled from 0, *no anxiety at all*, until 100, *extreme anxiety*. Then, this procedure was repeated for the second office room. All ratings were orally reported by the subject and noted by the experimenter. At the end of rating phase three, another rating slide was added requesting the US expectancy in the two rooms, respectively. Another scale ranging from 0 till 100 was shown, 0 representing *no expectation* of an electric shock and 100 representing *complete expectation* of US. Screenshots applied in this rating only served as labeling of the concerning context and were not used in the test-phase (supplement J).

After the EEG test-phase, participants saw each screenshot once again (12 CXT+US, 12 CXT+noUS and 24 CXT-) for 1000 ms and were asked whether a US was presented in the acquisition phase exactly at the time depicted in the screenshot. This part of the experiment was conducted with *Presentation* software (version 15.1, Neurobehavioral Systems, Inc.). Subjects typed their ratings on a 100-point scale into the computer by using a keyboard. 0 signified that *surely no US was presented* and 100 implied that participants *surely remembered an electric shock* at this position (supplement L).

The participants' last task was to assign each screenshot to one of the office rooms. Therefore, screenshots were presented again for 3000 ms with *Presentation* software (version 15.1, Neurobehavioral Systems, Inc.) and participants were asked to allocate the pictures to the context in which they were taken (supplement M).

2.3.2.2 Physiological recordings

Skin conductance level and electroencephalogram were recorded as objective and psychophysiological indicators of induced fear and anxiety.

2.3.2.2.1 Skin conductance level

During the acquisition phases, physiological reactions were measured by the subjects' skin conductance level. Measurements were taken by filling two 13/7 mm Ag-AgCl electrodes with 0.5% NaCl-paste and placing them on the thenar eminence and hypo-thenar eminence of the left non-dominant hand. Data collection was extended over pre-acquisition and acquisition phases 1 and 2, starting when a subject entered a room in virtual reality and ending when the participant was guided out of the room and into the corridor. Data was recorded via the software *Vision Recorder* (Brain Products GmbH, Munich, Germany) on a mobile notebook.

2.3.2.2.2 Electroencephalography

Event-related brain potentials (ERPs) were measured by applying an international 10-20 EEG system (Acticap, Brain Products GmbH, Munich, Germany). This 32-channel system consisted of 28 electrodes (Fp1, Fp2, F7, F3, Fz, F4, F8, FC5, FC1, FC2, FC6, T7, C3, Cz, C4, T8, CP5, CP1, CP2, CP6, P7, P3, Pz, P4, P8, O1, Oz, O2), which were fixed in a cap and located on the scalp. Additionally, four electrodes were placed directly in the subject's face to control for eye movements. Two electrodes were located on the left and right canthi to control for horizontal eye movements and two electrodes were fixed centrally above and beneath the right eye to record vertical eye movements. FCz was used as online reference and AFz as ground electrode. Impedances were kept below 5 kΩ using an electrolyte gel (EASYCAP GmbH, Herrsching, Germany) that connected the electrodes with the scalp in order to improve the signal-to-noise ratio. Impedances were checked with the *Acticap Control* software (version 1.2.2.0, Brain Products GmbH, Munich, Germany) and data were recorded using the *Vision Recorder* software (version 1.20, Brain Products GmbH, Munich, Germany). Sampling rate was set at 100 Hz.

2.4   Experimental procedure and design

2.4.1   The laboratory

The main experiment was conducted in the powerwall laboratory in the Department of Psychology I in Würzburg. The powerwall is a screen, 2 m in height and 3.22 m in length, and positioned on ground level of the laboratory. Virtual environment, all stimulus pictures and instructions were shown on this projector. The advantages of a presentation in a full-size environment with high resolution were an enhanced presence feeling and a greater involvement of the subjects in the virtual scenario. By this, physiological responses could be recorded in a highly controlled laboratory environment, but participants could react similar as in a real world situation.

2.4.2   Experimental design

Before the experiment, participants were assigned to one experimental procedure (supplement B). When participants arrived in the laboratory they signed informed consent (supplement D), read written instructions (supplement E) and completed the questionnaires. Subjects were always encouraged to ask questions, especially concerning the understanding of the experimental procedure and the rating scales.

As a first step, once seated in front of the powerwall the electrodes recording the electrodermal activity were applied at the subject's left non-dominant hand. Furthermore, a 32-channel EEG *Acticap* system was attached on the participant's head and gel filled into the electrodes to improve electric conductivity. After that their personal pain threshold was determined for the aversive electric stimuli applied in the conditioning phases.

During the experiment virtual reality was displayed on the powerwall. The experimental procedure was presented in *Half-Life 2* and controlled by the software *Cybersession* (version 5.3.38), which was developed in the Department of Psychology I, University of Würzburg. Figure 3 gives summary of the different blocks of the experimental design.

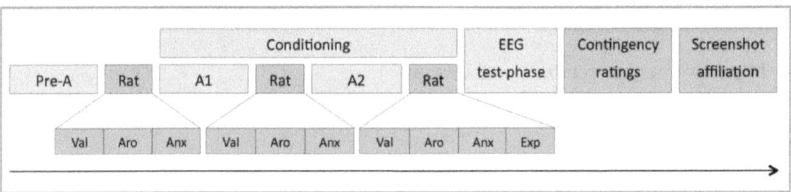

Figure 3: Overview of the experimental design: pre-acquisition (Pre-A), acquisition phase 1 (A1), acquisition phase 2 (A2), ratings (Rat) in between regarding to valence (Val), arousal (Aro), anxiety (Anx) and US-expectancy (Exp), followed by the EEG test-phase, contingency ratings and screenshot affiliation.

Recent contextual conditioning studies in humans use pre-exposure in terms of pre-acquisition phases to the contexts standardly due to subjects' habituation to the contexts and create a baseline measurement (e.g. Baas et al., 2008; Glotzbach-Schoon et al., 2013; Grillon, Cordova, Morgan, Charney & Davis., 2004). In the pre-acquisition phase, subjects were guided on the pre-recorded paths through each virtual office room. Afterwards, participants were asked to rate the office rooms in regard to valence, arousal and anxiety.

Two phases of acquisition followed during which the fear conditioning took place. Again, participants were guided through each of the office rooms in a pseudo-randomized order and perceived in one room between one and three electric shocks per trial in the dangerous (CXT+), but never in the safety context (CXT-). Phase one consisted of three trials per context, then, ratings appeared. Phase two was also composed of three trials per room and again the valence, arousal and anxiety ratings followed. Additionally, the expectancy of the US was asked in each room after the second acquisition phase to test the subjects' awareness of dangerous and safety context. In total, twelve USs were administered which never occurred twice at the same place in the anxiety context. As a last step in this phase, participants were asked in which room electric shocks occurred. This was an open question, so subjects could describe the distinct office until a room was clearly identifiable. Participants, who could not answer this question correctly, did not explicitly learn the association between US and a distinct context and had to be excluded from data analysis.

During the test phase 24 screenshots per context were presented using *Presentation* software (version 15.1, Neurobehavioral Systems, Inc.), each picture was shown three times and EEG was recorded. As mentioned above, 24 screenshots represented the safety context (CXT-), 12 screenshots showed the anxiety context at the moment of a US presentation in the acquisition phase (CXT+US), and 12 additional screenshots depicted the CXT+ at a moment when no US was given (CXT+noUS). In order to evoke event-related brain potentials, stimuli were separately shown for 1000 ms followed by an inter-trial interval, which lasted between 1500 ms and 2500 ms.

A contingency rating of all 48 screenshots followed in order to test the subjects' ability to differentiate screenshots of the two rooms and also their awareness of the places in the room where exactly an US was administered. The subjects' last task consisted of assigning every shown screenshot to one of the office rooms to clarify the definiteness of the screenshot categories.

At last, all devices were removed from the participants. Before they left the laboratory, subjects were paid and kindly thanked.

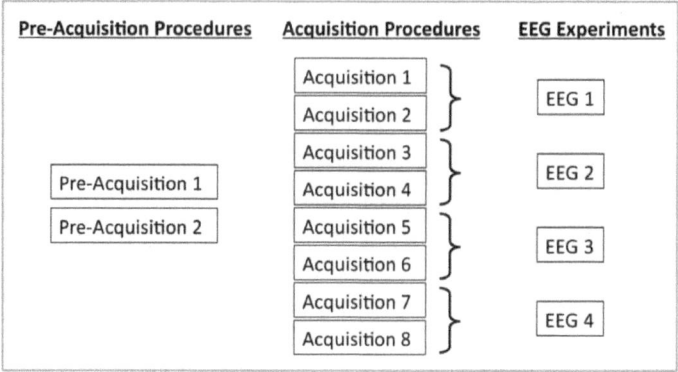

Figure 4: The different experimental procedures in order to counterbalance conditions over participants. Two pre-acquisition procedures, 8 acquisition procedures were randomized over participants. The 4 EEG Experiments only differed in the labeling of markers in regard to the respective acquisition procedure.

For the purpose of balancing the order of entering the rooms and assigning anxiety or safety contexts, different procedures were developed. Two pre-acquisition and eight acquisition procedures were designed, balancing the order of contexts in the pre-acquisition phase as well as anxiety or safety context and screenshots with or without US presentation in the acquisition (Fig. 4). Considering all of these aspects, a total number of 16 different experimental procedures were generated. One male and one female participant were randomly assigned to each procedure. A detailed sequence of the procedures is shown in the supplement (B, H, I).

2.5   Data reduction and analysis

When measuring participants 1-8 one US stimulus was not elicited in a particular trial of the acquisition phase with originally two US triggers. The data of these subjects were included in analyses, because on the one hand, data had no influence on results regarding to significant values, and on the other hand, the relevant trial still contained one elicited US and can therefore be regarded as fear conditioning trial. However, in EEG recordings as well as in contingency ratings, the particular stimulus was excluded for the eight participants.

In all analyses the alpha level was set at $p \leq .05$. In case of violating sphericity, Greenhouse-Geisser corrections $(GG\text{-}\varepsilon)$ in regard to the degrees of freedom were applied. Additionally, partial η^2 $(\eta_p{}^2)$ were reported (Picton et al., 2000).

2.5.1 Analysis of subjective data

Rating data were read in *SPSS* (version 20.0, IBM statistics, USA) and analyzed. For each rating, 2 x 3 repeated measurement Analyses of Variance (ANOVAs) were calculated respectively with the independent variables context (CXT+ and CXT-) and time (pre-acquisition, acquisition phase 1, acquisition phase 2). Additional *t*-tests were used to further analyze main effects and interactions.

The US-expectancy was rated after acquisition phase 2 and also analyzed in *SPSS* (version 20.0). Therefore, mean US-expectancies in CXT+ and CXT- were calculated in % and *t*-tests were calculated to assure the participant's successful learning of the association between context and US.

Contingency ratings between screenshots with US presentation and without were assessed. As an estimated value of 50 represented chance level, data were separately tested for each screenshot category (CXT+US, CXT+noUS, CXT-) via *t*-tests against 50.

Furthermore, the affiliation of each of the screenshots to the correct context was asked. A ceiling effect of high correctness of the answers was expected. Hence, mean subjects' percentage of right answers was calculated in order to get evidence for the definiteness of the screenshots. The 48 pictures should appear once and be presented in random order. However, due to an error in stimulus randomization concerning this part of the study, 48 screenshots appeared, but accidentally picked out of the stimulus pool. So, some screenshots were presented several times, some never. As each subject consequently rated a different selection of screenshots nevertheless, every single screenshot was rated many times, so data could be used for analyzing the definiteness of the stimuli.

2.5.2 Analysis of physiological data

2.5.2.1 Skin conductance level

Skin conductance measurements lasted throughout the whole conditioning phase. Data analysis was performed with the *Vision Analyzer* software (version 1.05.0005, Brain Products GmbH, Munich, Germany). At first, a low pass filter of 1 Hz was applied to the signal. Data were segmented, starting with entering a virtual room and ending with leaving the room, the door was used as trigger. Application of electric shocks in the anxiety context is associated with transient changes of skin conductance. For that reason, time intervals beginning from each US onset and ending 10 s after each US were excluded from SCL calculations. SCL values were transferred into *SPSS* (version 20.0) for statistical analysis and log-transformed in order to normalize data distribution (Chan & Lovibond, 1996). 2 x 3 repeated-measures ANOVAs with the inner subject factors context (CXT+ and CXT-) and time (pre-acquisition, acquisition phase 1, acquisition phase 2) were calculated. Main effects were further analyzed with *t*-tests.

2.5.2.2 Electroencephalography

Amplitudes of the ERP components P100, EPN and LPP were calculated and compared between the screenshot categories. In respect to the analysis, as a first step data were preprocessed to extract the recorded EEG signal from noise. The *Vision Analyzer* software (version 1.05.0005, Brain Products GmbH, Munich, Germany) was used. A bandpass filter from 0.1 Hz to 35 Hz was applied as well as a Notch filter of 50 Hz. Ocular corrections were performed over all channels using the electrodes placed around the subjects' eyes (17, 22, 28, 32) via the automatic correction implemented in *Vision Analyzer* (Gratton, Coles & Donchin, 1983). After that, a new reference was calculated using all electrodes except the two frontal electrodes (1 and 2) that were defect and except the eye electrodes. In order to get single trial signals, data were segmented in 1200 ms intervals lasting from 200 ms before until 1000 ms after stimulus onset. Subsequently, an artifact rejection was performed that allowed a maximal voltage step of 50 µV, a minimal amplitude of -100 µV and a maximal amplitude of 100 µV. Also, baseline correction was conducted beginning 100 ms before stimulus onset and ending with stimulus presentation. Segmentation and averaging of all three kinds of stimuli (CXT+US, CXT+noUS, CXT-) followed afterwards. In terms of analyzing the P100 component, peak detection was performed in a time interval of 100-150 ms. Values of these peaks were exported into *SPSS* for statistical analyses. In particular, the values of electrodes O1 and O2 were included in the P100 analysis.

For the purpose of analyzing the EPN and LPP components, area detections were implemented from 240-280 ms and from 400-600 ms, respectively. These values were also transferred into *SPSS* (version 20.0). Regarding to the EPN, electrodes O1, O2, P7 and P8 were analyzed and for the LPP the Pz electrode was taken into account. There, repeated-measures ANOVAs were calculated for each component, separately. For the LPP analysis, the within subject factor context (CXT+, CXT-) was calculated to investigate the contextual conditioning procedure and additionally an ANOVA was calculated with the within-subject factor screenshot category (CXT+US, CXT+noUS, CXT-) for the description of context and cue conditioning. For the P100 the hemispheric effect was additionally calculated. Therefore, 2 x 2 repeated measures ANOVA were performed containing the within subject factors context (CXT+, CXT-) and hemisphere (left, right) as well as 3 x 2 repeated measures ANOVAs including the within factors screenshot category (CXT+US, CXT+noUS, CXT-) and hemisphere (left, right). For the EPN, hemisphere (left, right), electrode location (parietal, occipital) and screenshot category were investigated calculating a 2 x 2 x 3 repeated measure ANOVA. Significant main effects and interactions were further tested using *t*-tests.

2.5.3 Explorative analyses

Gender effects were analyzed by adding the between-subject factor gender to the ANOVAs of each ERP component, respectively. Furthermore, as in David Meyer-Heintze's study (2011) an effect of EEG amplitudes could only be found when the office with red carpet served as anxiety context, the between-subject factor context was also added to the ERP analysis.

In order to investigate the influence of the participants' general anxiety and personal characteristics on the conditioning effect and ERP amplitudes, Pearson's correlations were calculated. Questionnaires in particular the Positive and Negative

Affect Schedule (PANAS; Watson et al., 1988; German version by Krohne et al., 1996), the anxiety sensitivity index (ASI; Reiss et al., 1986; German version by Alpers & Pauli, 2001), the Behavioral Inhibition System and Behavioral Approach System questionnaire (BIS/BAS; Carver & White, 1994; German version by Strobel et al., 2001) and the State-Trait-Anxiety-Inventory (Spielberger et al., 1970; German version by Laux et al., 1981) and EEG data (values of P100, EPN, LPP) were read into *SPSS* (version 20.0) and correlated. Additionally, correlations of questionnaires and valence, arousal and anxiety levels were calculated. Moreover, questionnaires were correlated with US-expectancy ratings in terms of revealing coherence between the subjects' anxiety level and the ability to learn context-US associations.

3 Results

3.1 Sample characteristics

In total, 32 participants took part in the study and went through the complete experimental procedure. Four participants did not learn the association between anxiety context and US and safety context without US, and therefore were regarded as unaware and excluded from analysis. Twenty-eight subjects were able to correctly answer the open question about the context in which an electric shock was applied. They were assigned as aware, so their data were used for analyses.

Before conditioning, participants signed written informed consent and completed several questionnaires: PANAS (Positive And Negative Affect Schedule; Watson et al., 1988; German version by Krohne et al., 1996), ASI (Anxiety Sensitivity Index; Reiss et al., 1986; German version by Alpers & Pauli, 2001), BIS/BAS (Behavioral Inhibition System and Behavioral Activation System; Carver & White, 1994; German version by Strobel et al., 2001), STAI-state and -trait (State-Trait-Anxiety-Inventory; Spielberger et al., 1970; German version by Laux et al., 1981). Descriptive statistics including mean scores and standard deviations are presented in Table 2.

Table 2: Mean scores (*M*) and standard deviation (*SD*) on the questionnaires rated by the analyzed sample of 28 participants.

	M	*SD*
PANAS positive affect	32.11	6.51
PANAS negative affect	12.46	3.41
ASI	18.1	9.69
BIS	2.78	0.52
BAS	3.05	0.34
STAI state	36.11	8.20
STAI trait	36.68	9.15

Participants had a normal anxiety level according to the norm population. Even single data observation for each individual did not give any suspicion of very high anxiety or exaggerated positive or negative mood.

3.2   The unconditioned stimulus

The subjects' individual pain threshold was determined in the procedure mentioned above. On average, 2.01 mA $(SD = 1.09)$ were chosen as current intensity for the US. Participants assessed the pain intensity with a mean value of 5.96 $(SD = 0.92)$ on the 10-point scale (four indicated *just perceptible pain*). Additionally, valence and arousal were rated on the 100-point scale each. The electric stimulus was evaluated with a mean valence of 36.7 $(SD = 18.9)$. Assuming that a score of 50 meant neutral and below 50 indicated negative feelings, t-tests against the neutral value of 50 showed a significant negative valence of the US, $t(27) = -3.87$, $p = .001$. In parallel, subjects stated a mean value of 58.0 $(SD = 18.7)$ on the 100-point arousal scale.

All in all, one can assume that the unconditioned stimuli indeed were aversive and moderately painful and evoked a feeling of unpleasantness as well as high arousal in each person that was included in analyses.

3.3   Explicit ratings

Explicit ratings of valence, arousal and anxiety were assessed three times: after pre-acquisition, after acquisition phase 1 and after acquisition phase 2. Moreover, US-expectancy was requested after acquisition phase 2 (see Fig. 3). Descriptive statistics of mean values (M) and standard deviations (SD) are depicted in Table 3.

Table 3: Rating scores after pre-acquisition, acquisition phase 1 and acquisition phase 2, mean values (*M*) and standard deviation (*SD*).

	CXT+		CXT-	
	M	*SD*	*M*	*SD*
Valence				
Pre-Acquisition	58.04	15.95	64.46	14.87
Acquisition Phase 1	33.39	15.99	69.82	15.78
Acquisition Phase 2	28.04	18.68	73.32	16.89
Arousal				
Pre-Acquisition	22.14	18.83	20.00	18.71
Acquisition Phase 1	60.36	18.75	33.39	21.43
Acquisition Phase 2	61.61	20.91	21.25	17.51
Anxiety				
Pre-Acquisition	7.68	15.37	6.25	11.60
Acquisition Phase 1	46.00	24.65	23.39	24.12
Acquisition Phase 2	45.36	23.84	10.54	14.36
US-Expectancy				
Acquisition Phase 2	91.79	12.64	11.79	14.09

3.3.1 Valence

The ANOVA revealed main effects of context, $F(1,27) = 79.808$, $p < .001$ $\eta_p^2 = .721$, and time, $F(2,54) = 14.019$, $p < .001$, $\eta_p^2 = .342$, GG-$\varepsilon = .825$, as well as an interaction effect Context x Time, $F(2,54) = 39.138$, $p < .001$, $\eta_p^2 = .592$, GG-$\varepsilon = .750$. Comparing contexts after pre-acquisition, paired t-test showed no significant difference between the valence of CXT+ and CXT-, $t(27) = -1.819$, $p = .080$. However, already after acquisition phase 1,valence ratings for CXT+ were significantly more negative compared to CXT-, $t(27) = -9.597$, $p < .001$. After the second acquisition phase the conditioning effect was even further enhanced, $t(27) = -8.083$, $p < .001$ (Fig. 5A). In sum, data showed that participants' pleasantness increased in the safety context, but it decreased in the anxiety context.

3.3.2 Arousal

The situation is similar with rating data of arousal. Repeated measure 2 x 3 ANOVA pointed out main effects of context, $F(1,27) = 124.430; p < .001; \eta_p^2 = .822$, and time, $F(2,54) = 32.213, p < .001, \eta_p^2 = .544, GG\text{-}\varepsilon = .790$, and interactions of Context x Time, $F(2,54) = 28.124, p < .001, \eta_p^2 = .510$. Paired t-tests elucidated no differences of arousal in the anxiety and safety context after pre-acquisition, $t(27) = 1.441, p = .161$. Regarding to both acquisition phases, participants significantly interpreted the anxiety context more arousing compared to the safety context in phase 1, $t(27) = 6.536, p < .001$, and phase 2, $t(27) = 8.928, p < .001$ (Fig. 5B).

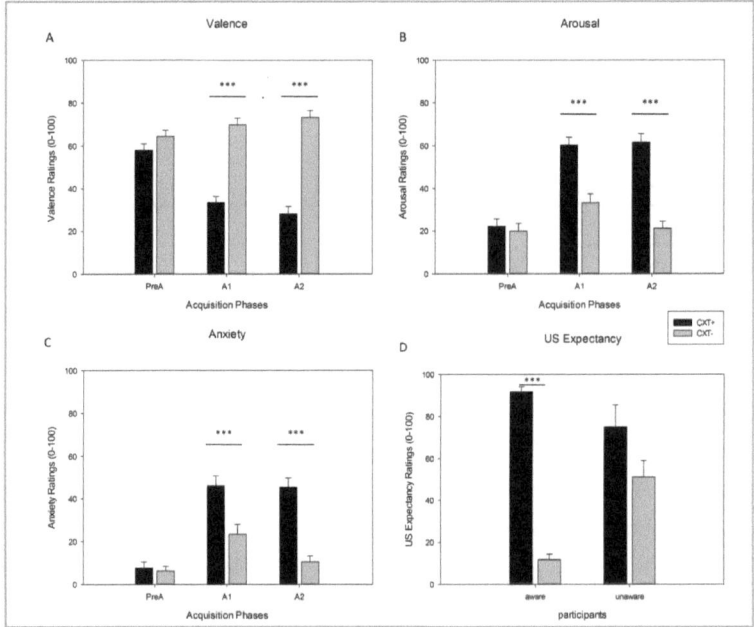

Figure 5: Explicit ratings of valence (A), arousal (B) and anxiety (C) in CXT+ and CXT- after pre-acquisition (PreA), acquisition phase 1 (A1) and acquisition phase 2 (A2). D depicts the US-expectancy ratings in CXT+ and CXT- after acquisition phase 2 separated in US aware and unaware participants.

3.3.3 Anxiety

Even concerning the third rating scale of anxiety, analysis of variance was applied. Again, repeated measure 2 x 3 ANOVA was calculated. Results indicated significant main effects of context, $F(1,27) = 85.536$, $p < .001$, $\eta_p^2 = .760$, and time, $F(2,54) = 29.845$, $p < .001$, $\eta_p^2 = .525$, and an interaction effect of Context x Time, $F(2,54) = 26.191$, $p < .001$, $\eta_p^2 = .492$. Additionally, paired t-tests revealed no differences in the subjects' anxiety in both rooms after pre-acquisition, $t(27) = 1.441$, $p = .161$. Besides, after acquisition phases 1 and 2, participants rated their level of anxiety higher in the anxiety context than in the safety context (phase 1: $t(27) = 6.046$, $p < .001$; phase 2: $t(27) = 7.722$, $p < .001$) (Fig. 5C).

To sum up, one can conclude that the context in which electric stimuli were applied evoked lower valence, more arousal and a higher level of anxiety compared to the safety context.

3.3.4 US-Expectancy

The last question in this part of the experiment affected the subjects' expectancy to perceive an electric shock. Participants rated 0, when they absolutely did not expect an US in the shown context, and 100, when they surely expected US administration. In terms of the safety context, the 28 aware participants estimated the likelihood of US administration with 11.8% on average ($SD = 14.1$). In contrast, the probability to perceive an electric stimulus in the anxiety context was indicated with a mean of 91.8% ($SD = 12.6$), which was significantly higher than for CXT-, $t(27) = 18.142$, $p < .001$. Again, statistics proofed that aware participants expected an US more likely in the anxiety compared to the safety context. Data is depicted in Figure 5D, on the left side.

But one has to emphasize that only aware participants are included in the data analyses. T-tests of the US-expectancy ratings against the chance value of 50 also revealed significant differences for CXT+, $t(27) = 17.499$, $p < .001$, and CXT-, $t(27) = -14.351$, $p < .001$.

The right part in Figure 5D additionally shows US expectancies rated by the four unaware subjects. Expectancy of an US in CXT+ was rated with $M = 75.0\%$ ($SD = 20.8$) and in CXT- with $M = 51.3\%$ ($SD = 15.5$). Though data observations appear different, paired t-tests showed no significant difference between ratings of anxiety and safety context, $t(3) = 1.358$, $p = .267$. Therefore, it was suggested that these participants did not learn the associations between electric shocks in a distinct environment and justifies data exclusion of the subjects.

3.3.5   Contingency ratings

After EEG-measurement, participants observed the screenshots again which were used in the test-phase (see Fig. 3). Their task was to estimate if they perceived an electric stimulus in the conditioning phase exactly at that very moment when the picture was taken. Subjects' answers, which ranged from 0 (*surely no US was administered*) to 100 (*surely there was an US administered*), were given via a keyboard. Importantly, a rating of 50 signified no tendency at all. So, data were tested in t-tests with one sample against the value of 50 for all three screenshot categories CXT+US, CXT+noUS and CXT-. As Figure 6 demonstrates, screenshots depicting the safety context were rarely associated with an US. Data point out a clear difference between the US ratings and 50, $t(27) = -22.677$, $p < .001$.

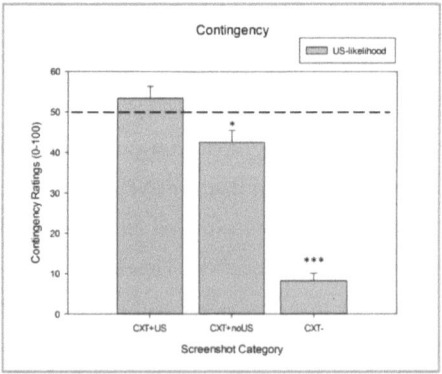

Figure 6: Contingency ratings of US expectancy of the participants at the time when the screenhots were taken separated in categories CXT+US, CXT+noUS and CXT-. T-tests against the chance value of 50 (-----): $p < .05$: *; p < .001: *.**

In general, ratings of the estimation of the US likelihood when presenting screenshots taken in the anxiety context were increased. Interestingly, screenshots of the CXT+ without any US administration were rated as significantly less associated with the US compared to 50, $t(27)$ = -2.553, p = .017, but screenshots of the CXT+ where USs were definitely given could not be assigned to a US greater than chance level, $t(27)$ = -1.139, p = .265 (Fig. 6).

3.3.6 Context ratings

The participants' very last task in the whole experiment (see Fig. 3) was to assign all previously presented stimuli to one of both office rooms. One picture after the other was referred to the offices in a forced-choice task to assess the definiteness of the selected stimuli. This was necessary to exclude ambiguity errors of the stimuli because furniture in the two rooms were similar. On an individual descriptive level of analysis, only four participants per room had a hit ratio of less than 90% per room and on an overall analysis, subjects dedicated pictures to the right office room with an overall accuracy of more than 95.1%. So the conclusion can be drawn that all participants included in data analysis were able to clearly differentiate the screenshots taken of both rooms.

3.4 Physiological Data

3.4.1 Electrodermal activity

Electrodermal activity was recorded during pre-acquisition and conditioning and is presented as skin conductance level (SCL). One participant had to be excluded because of incorrect marker positions. For that reason, 27 remaining participants were added in following analysis. Data were edited as described above and log-transformed. Descriptive statistics are shown in Table 4.

Table 4: Log-transformed data of skin conductance level in acquisition phases, mean values (*M*) and standard deviation (*SD*).

	CXT+		CXT-	
	M	*SD*	*M*	*SD*
SCL				
Pre-Acquisition	0.502	0.190	0.498	0.190
Acquisition Phase 1	0.532	0.196	0.515	0.191
Acquisition Phase 2	0.498	0.208	0.486	0.201

Statistical analysis in terms of repeated measure 2 x 3 ANOVA was performed containing the inner-subject factors context (CXT+ and CXT-) and time (pre-acquisition, acquisition phase 1 and acquisition phase 2). Results indicated main effects of context, $F(1,26) = 15.269$, $p = .001$, $\eta_p^2 = .375$ and time, $F(2,52) = 5.081$, $p = .010$, $\eta_p^2 = .163$, but no interaction effect. Similar to the results of the ratings, explorative analyses showed that CXT+ and CXT- did not differ during pre-acquisition when participants were passing through the two office rooms, $t(26) = .574$, $p = .571$. When exploring acquisition phase 1, a distinct differentiation between anxiety and safety context arose, $t(26) = 3.109$, $p = .005$ in terms of significantly enhanced SCL in CXT+ compared to CXT-. The effect is also visible but less exposed in acquisition phase 2, $t(26) = 2.130$, $p = .043$ (Figure 7).

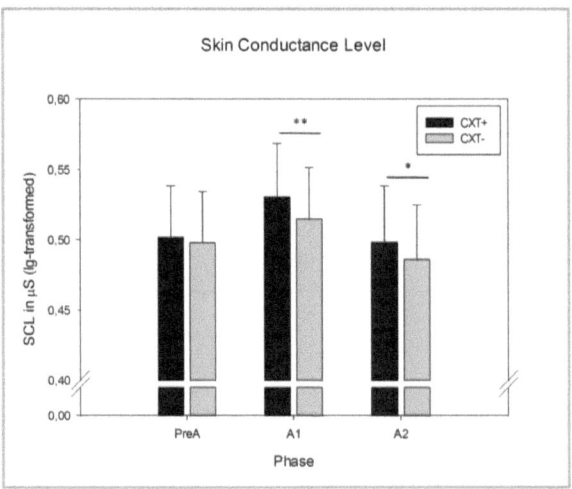

Figure 7: Skin conductance level in CXT+ and CXT- during pre-acquisition (PreA), during acquisition phase 1 (A1) and during acquisition phase 2 (A2). Statistics compared SCL in CXT+ with SCL in CXT-, $p < .05$: *; $p < .01$: **.

3.4.2 Electroencephalography

Event-related brain potentials were evoked by visually presented screenshots categorized in CXT+US, CXT+noUS and CXT-. The four unaware as well as one additional participant who was assigned to an incorrect EEG procedure were excluded. As one US in one experimental procedure was not administered, this stimulus had to be excluded from analyses for participants 1 to 8. This exclusion had no impact on statistical analysis. Components P100, EPN and LPP were analyzed separately. Descriptive statistics are depicted in Table 5, presenting mean values (M) of electrical potentials of component relevant electrodes and the standard error (SE). The peak value of electrical potential in regard to the P100 was displayed, and concerning the analyzed time window for the EPN and LPP, values of electrical potentials were averaged.

Table 5: Mean EEG values (*M*) in μV and standard error (*SE*). P100: value with the highest amplitude located via peak detection; EPN and LPP: values calculated as mean amplitude over the selected time interval.

	CXT+US		CXT+noUS		CXT-	
	M	*SE*	*M*	*SE*	*M*	*SE*
P100						
O1	6.613	0.681	6.756	0.609	6.491	0.562
O2	7.268	0.898	7.672	0.856	7.090	0.736
EPN						
O1	7.590	0.958	7.437	0.927	7.484	0.854
O2	7.917	1.095	8.270	1.063	8.057	0.914
P7	3.513	0.511	3.705	0.662	3.312	0.441
P8	4.690	0.577	4.850	0.554	4.977	0.519
LPP						
Pz	1.918	0.469	2.052	0.450	1.957	0.483

3.4.2.1 P100

Analyzing the P100 component, occipital electrodes O1 and O2 were included. Repeated measure 2 x 3 ANOVA contained the inner-subject factors hemisphere (left and right) and screenshot category (CXT+US, CXT+noUS and CXT-). No main effects, neither for screenshot condition, $F(1,26) = .088$, $p = .916$, $\eta_p^2 = .003$, nor for hemisphere, $F(1,26) = 3.713$, $p = .065$, $\eta_p^2 = .125$, could be revealed. However, a slight tendency of stronger ERP amplitude at the right compared to the left occipital cortex was observed. In order to get a clue about any physiological reaction in the EEG signal concerning context conditioning, additionally all P100 amplitudes evoked by screenshots depicting the anxiety context were averaged (CXT+US and CXT+noUS) and compared to the safety context. Nevertheless, the ANOVA suggested no significant differences in EEG amplitudes for CXT+ and CXT-, $F(1,26) = .119$, $p = .732$, $\eta_p^2 = .004$.

3.4.2.2 EPN

The early posterior negativity was analyzed over occipital electrodes O1 and O2 and additionally over parietal electrodes P7 and P8. Repeated measure 2 x 2 x 3 ANOVA was applied with the inner-subject factors hemisphere (left and right), electrode location (parietal and occipital) and screenshot category (CXT+US, CXT+noUS and CXT-). Analysis of screenshot category was far from any significance ($F(2,52) = 0.252$, $p = .778$, $\eta_p^2 = .010$). However, a main effect of hemisphere could be shown with an increased amplitude at the right compared to the left hemisphere, $F(1,26) = 6.697$, $p = .016$, $\eta_p^2 = .205$. Moreover, a main effect of electrode location was revealed with an enhanced occipital compared to parietal signal, $F(1,26) = 30.406$, $p < .001$, $\eta_p^2 = .010$, could be shown. In Figure 8, ERP signals are displayed for all four relevant electrodes with highlighted analyzed time window between 240 and 280 ms.

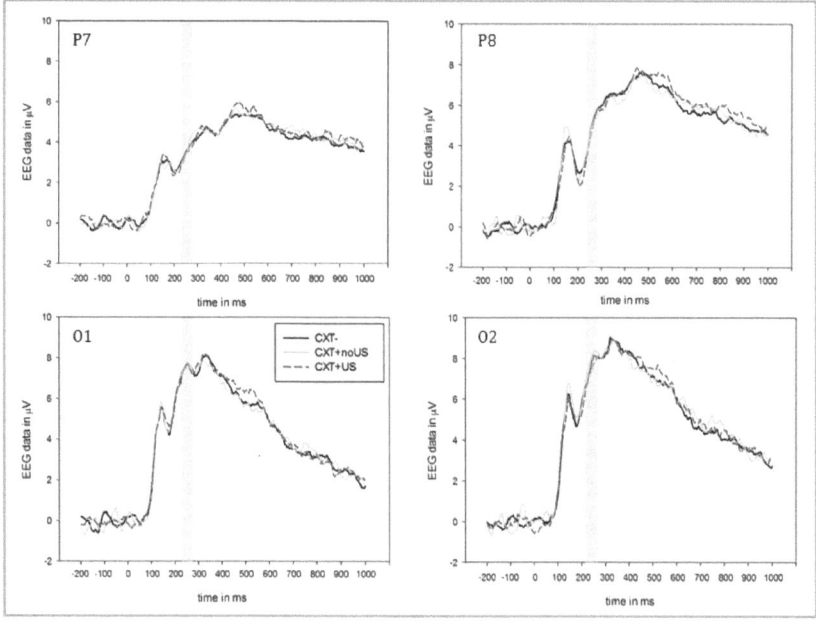

Figure 8: Event-related potentials elicited by screenshots of the three categories CXT+US, CXT+noUS and CXT- of the four analyzed electrodes P7, P8, O1 and O2. Highlighted is the time interval between 240 and 280 ms in which the EPN was analyzed.

Concerning only the whole anxiety context (CXT+US and CXT+noUS) revealed no difference between CXT+ and CXT-, main effect of screenshot category, $F(1,26) = .058$, $p = .811$, $\eta_p^2 = .002$. Analyzing data on a contextual level, data of CXT+US and CXT+noUS were pooled to one anxiety context data set. Comparison of this data with CXT- revealed no difference between CXT+ and CXT-.

3.4.2.3 LPP

Visual inspection of the late positive potential at electrode Pz revealed a poorly pronounced ERP component. Nevertheless, repeated measure ANOVA with the inner-subject factor screenshot category (CXT+US, CXT+noUS and CXT-) was performed. Data revealed no main effect suggesting no significant differences in the EEG signal between the three categories, $F(1,26) = 1.322$, $p = .276$, $\eta_p^2 = .048$. Even on a contextual conditioning level comparing CXT+ (CXT+US and CXT+noUS) and CXT-, the ANOVA did not reach significance, $F(1,26) = 1.843$, $p = .184$, $\eta_p^2 = .056$.

3.5 Explorative analyses

Further analyses were performed to reveal any effects of gender or context. Therefore, gender was added as group variable into the ANOVAs for ERP data, but neither influenced the P100 nor the EPN nor the LPP (all $ps > .703$). In the same way, the effect of the two office rooms serving as anxiety or safety context respectively, was revealed by extending ANOVA of the EEG data with the group variable of context (room 1 vs. room 2). Here, no effects could be demonstrated in which the context influenced any event-related potential amplitude (all $ps > .296$).

Besides, correlations between EEG data and questionnaires as well as US-contingency ratings and questionnaires were of interest. Therefore, Pearson's correlation was calculated. For comparing EEG and questionnaires, the differences between ERP amplitudes between CXT+US, CXT+noUS and CXT- were calculated separately and correlated with all questionnaire sum scores (PANAS positive affect, PANAS negative affect, ASI, BIS, BAS, STAI-tait, STAI-state). But p-values were higher than .079 (|Pearson's r| < .338) and therefore one can conclude that scores in questionnaires, indicating the subjects' emotional state, mood and anxiety, did not influence EEG amplitudes.

Moreover, Pearson's correlations between questionnaires and mean context ratings during both acquisition phases were calculated.

As data clearly proofed no differences in valence, arousal and anxiety level between acquisition phase 1 and 2, data were summarized to one conditioning data set for valence, arousal and anxiety, respectively, for correlation analyses.

First, the mean values of valence, arousal and anxiety in CXT+ and CXT- were assessed, respectively. Then in each rating differences between CXT+ and CXT- served as value used in correlation analysis. However, correlations of questionnaires and valence are far from significance (all $ps > .093$) as well as arousal (all $ps > .371$) and anxiety (all $ps > .072$) ($|$Pearson's $r| < .338$).

Furthermore, Pearson's correlations between US-expectancy ratings and questionnaires were calculated over all 28 participants. Data should give information, whether subjective emotional states influenced contextual conditioning. Hence, differences between US expectancies in CXT+ and CXT- were calculated and used for correlation analysis. But data indicated no correlation at all (all $ps > .154$) and therefore suggested that learning the awareness of anxiety context and US is not influenced by characteristics of the subjects' personality.

4 Discussion

In this study, the influence of cues in a classical contextual fear conditioning paradigm was investigated. The experimental design was already used in David Meyer-Heintze's diploma thesis (2011), however the main goal here was to control stimuli in a wider extent and therefore to be able to draw conclusions about the development of fear and anxiety afterwards.

While contextual fear conditioning was successfully conducted in virtual reality established by subjective ratings and skin conductance level analysis, there was no evidence at all for cue and contextual conditioning measured in ERP amplitudes.

4.1 The virtual environments

Firstly, we could prepare virtual environments in advance serving for a specific purpose, in this case the creation of two virtual rooms, which were equal in valence, arousal, complexity, and screenshots of the rooms that had additionally the same picture properties like entropy and RGB-value. Therefore, the two contexts were highly controlled. Many studies already used VR in conditioning experiments (Alvarez et al., 2008; Baas et al., 2004; Grillon, Baas, Cornwell & Johnson, 2006) and did not report any selective controlling of stimuli. They used skin conductance response and fear-potentiated startle reflex rather than EEG recordings, which are both not as susceptible for physical properties as ERPs. In many cases, virtual environments depicted highly different scenarios like restaurant, casino and bank (Alvarez et al., 2008) or one apartment containing several rooms (Baas et al., 2008). Meyer-Heintze (2011) used EEG for the first time and aimed at investigating cue conditioning parallel to contextual conditioning, which should be improved but not be validated with the recent experiment.

4.2 Choosing the kind of unconditioned stimuli

Regarding the procedure of conditioning, one also has to reflect the kind of US, which was applied in this study. Hugdahl & Johnsen (1989) discussed the use of electric shocks for painful stimulation. Aversive noise like a loud scream was also frequently applied

(Barrett & Armony, 2009) which generally provide a great method to induce anxiety. Less often, human experiments use aversive odors as US. This is due to the fact that it is harder to determine the different sensitivities towards odors in humans and that the sense of smelling is less developed in humans than in rodents or insects. In conditioning experiments with bees, odors provide a great stimulus for aversive or appetitive conditioning (Matsumoto et al., 2012).

However, in recent experiment, electric shocks were applied. A main advantage was the individual pain threshold that could be determined before the experiment was started. This might explain why on one hand all participants rated the US as painful and on the other hand no subject interrupted or canceled the experiment early.

4.3 Contextual fear conditioning

Classical fear conditioning to one particular virtual context was successfully performed. The associative learning was mainly indexed by a very higher US-expectancy rating in the anxiety compared to the safety context. But one has to emphasize that only US aware participants were included in the analysis. The four unaware subjects were not able to distinguish the anxiety from the safety context, although at the beginning of the experiment participants were instructed to pay attention to the predictability of the US. However, as both office rooms were built in the same map of the Hammer Editor, and seemed to be located in the identical building, it might have been hard for some individuals to consciously follow where exactly in the virtual environment they were located. Even the kind how the rooms were built concerning the furniture was similar as both were offices, which made the differentiation more difficult. Generally, many studies (e.g. Baas et al., 2004; Glotzbach-Schoon et al., 2013; Meyer-Heintze, 2011), which investigated conditioning, reported that some subjects did not learn the CS-US associations. Here, unawareness might have occurred as an effect of a lack of participants' attention and alertness during the experiment.

As Lang described (1995), subjective ratings are one of the three levels of the motivational defense system to measure anxiety besides behavioral and physiological reactions. Frequently, subjective ratings were assessed as an indicator for contextual conditioning, which is also very useful to investigate subjective feelings as a function of time (Baas et al., 2008; Grillon et al., 2006).

In the pre-acquisition phase of the recent study baseline ratings of aware subjects suggested that both virtual rooms were estimated as evoking equal levels of valence, arousal and anxiety. This is not surprising, as the pilot study described earlier, was conducted to control virtual environment conditions for exactly these aspects. Besides, experimental procedures in terms of CXT+ and CXT- were randomized. For that reasons any effect of the context itself could be excluded.

Already after the first acquisition phase all ratings differed highly significant between anxiety and safety context. These effects remained on the same level, even after acquisition phase 2. Here, it could also be shown that fear conditioning worked very rapidly, since after three guided tours through each room and the administration of only six aversive electric stimuli in the anxiety context, subjects' ratings clearly identified the context linked to the threat.

Moreover, physiological measurements of skin conductance, which is a very common method in assessing conditioning (Sehlmeyer et al., 2009), also proofed contextual fear conditioning. Hamm & Weike (2005) attributed skin conductance to contingency learning because explicit stimulus awareness is necessary to evoke physiological changes in the skin. In the pre-acquisition phase, skin conductance level was equal in CXT+ and CXT-. After acquisition phase 1, SCL increased in general, because subjects were instructed that electric shocks would be administered in this phase of the experiment. In this part difference in SCL was greatest between CXT+ and CXT-. Enhanced skin conductivity was associated with increased arousal in terms of a sympathetic nerve system that is activated to be able to respond very fast and appropriate (Bradley, 2009; Fenz & Eppstein, 1967).

Joseph LeDoux (2012) explained the reaction to threat that elicits increased arousal on a cellular level. Sensory inputs, e.g. auditory, visual or odor cues, activate neurons of lateral followed by central amygdala neurons. These neurons target dendritic areas of norepinephrine, dopamine, serotonin and acetylcholine containing neurons. Due to their activation these transmitters are released. Additionally, neuronal outputs from the central amygdala are transferred to further neurons that activate the sympathetic nerve system and initiate hormonal stress response. In particular, adrenergic hormones are released via the adrenal medulla and cortisol is released via the activated hypothalamic-pituitary-adrenal axis. Furthermore, LeDoux (2012) discussed the specificity of an activated arousal mechanism for facilitated processing of external stimuli (Hurley, Devilbiss & Waterhouse, 2004), enhanced attention, the involvement in memory processes (Roozendaal et al., 2009) and at least the whole survival circuit. From this neuronal point of view, one can conclude that various mechanisms of physiological arousal indicated by changes in skin conductance level contribute to prepare an organism for threatening and survival relevant situations.

Having a closer look at acquisition phase 2, the SCL decreased in total and also the difference between anxiety and safety context decreased from highly significant to a significant level. A reason for that might be habituation, which depends on a repeated activation of a certain stimulated pathway (Aguilar, 2003). Responses to this particular stimulus attenuate. Eric Kandel investigated habituation in terms of defense reflexes on a neurobiological level in the model organism *aplysia* regarding to its gill and siphon withdrawal reflex. Castellucci & Kandel (1974) found a decreased post-synaptic potential and reduced neurotransmitter release due to habituation. Moreover, the habituation effect is also well known in humans for example in startle response (Bradley, Lang & Cuthbert, 1993) or perception of painful stimulation (Rhudy, Bartley & Williams, 2010).

So far, it can be concluded that the contextual conditioning part of the recent study in VR worked on a physiological and subjective level. Therefore, the first hypothesis about contextual conditioning in virtual reality could be verified.

4.4   Cue conditioning

The second and even more interesting research question of this study concerned the cue conditioning effect, a model for fear and fear disorders like specific phobias (Craske et al., 2009). Therefore, contingency awareness between screenshots of the anxiety context with and without US presentation has to be discussed. We hypothesized cue conditioning without participants' awareness of stimuli representing CXT+US and CXT+noUS. However, ERP recordings turned out to be a measurement not suitable enough to represent neither cue nor contextual conditioning.

Awareness was assessed by asking participants, whether they perceived an electric shock at the presented particular locations in the virtual environment. Subjects rated their sureness from 0 (*surely no US*) until 100 (*surely US*). As 50 meant absolutely no idea about the likelihood of US administration, the CS-US contingency could be revealed by calculation of the relative distance of ratings to chance level (50).

Data displayed ratings lower than chance for the estimated likelihood of US-administration in the safety context. One can draw the conclusion that participants were able to clearly distinguish screenshots depicting the safety context from screenshots showing the anxiety context. This was not obvious, because Meyer-Heintze (2011) used office rooms with very prominent carpet colors of red and green, which at first glance seem much easier to differentiate rather than the new adapted virtual office rooms with carpet colors depicting two shades of red (see Fig. 2). Nevertheless, the new screenshots showed the same rating pattern regarding to CXT+US and CXT+noUS as in the diploma thesis (Meyer-Heintze, 2011). However, ratings for screenshots depicting CXT- were not investigated before. Here, the ratings for screenshots showing CXT+US were not significantly different from the chance value of 50. Pictures depicting CXT+noUS were rated significantly below 50, which could be associated with an easier recall of screenshots representing the anxiety context at a moment without US application. An explanation might be that the analyzed aware participants memorized few CXT+US screenshots where they surely perceived an US. However, subjects rated all other pictures, where they were unsure about CS-US contingency slightly below 50. The few CXT+US that were rated with certainty were too few to differ significantly from 50, so this screenshot category had an overall US estimation of chance level. When participants observed screenshots that they could not surely assign to either CXT+US or CXT+noUS, subjects rated them with a value of below 50. This could be the reason, why CXT+noUS were rated significantly below the value of 50. Due to the fact that all screenshots were preselected in the pilot-study and counterbalanced in serving as CXT+US or CXT+noUS, the effect of distinct forms or parts of the room that are easier to remember can be excluded.

From this perspective, one can conclude that subjects showed almost no contingency awareness of the stimuli used for the EEG test-phase and the US administration. This was expected as it is very hard to learn in which exact moment an

US was once applied. These confirm the hypothesis of the participants' unawareness of stimulus-US contingencies. Subsequently, cue conditioning was assessed.

As first and obvious explanation, one could claim that no cue conditioning took place at all. This could clearly be verified looking at the investigated ERP amplitudes evoked by screenshots of CXT+US and CXT+noUS, which were on the same level even with amplitudes evoked by pictures depicting the safety context (CXT-). When pooling screenshot categories to a contextual conditioning level, in particular to CXT+ and CXT-, and comparing the amplitudes, no difference could be seen, too. However, contextual conditioning was proven by ratings and skin conductance, as discussed above, but was not depicted in ERP amplitudes. Since context conditioning could be proven on all levels except on the level of brain activity, the absence of differing EEG amplitudes due to the screenshot categories cannot serve as an explanation that cue conditioning does not take place.

A second possibility, why we don't see distinct ERPs, could be due to the cues themselves. Marschner et al.'s (2008) conditioning study with functional magnetic resonance imaging (fMRI) used pictures of rooms as background and very distinct geometric figures as conditioned stimuli that appeared in the centre of the picture. The difference between background context and discrete CS that predicted the US, clearly proofed cue conditioning in terms of increased amygdala activity as a response to the CS+ compared to the CS-. Another study (Grillon et al., 2006) used light panels as conditioned stimuli. On the one hand, light is a stimulus that is integrated better into the background context and therefore more difficult to associate with a US. On the other hand, colored light does not provide stimuli that appear completely natural in the virtual context the participants are transferred to. However, this study also gives evidence for cue conditioning, as participants showed increased startle response when a cue predicted the shock compared to a context without cue presentation. Baas et al. (2008) also revealed that context conditioning, in terms of an increased reaction to the anxiety compared to the safety context, occurs, whenever no specific cue is associated with the US. In contrast, cue conditioning and only diminished contextual conditioning took place, when subjects learned to associate a distinct cue with the US. The conditioning experiments discussed above also contained pre-acquisition, acquisition and test phase similar to recent study. The question remains, whether cue conditioning even occurs when the relevant stimulus is an integrated part of the context. If the stimulus is perceived as a US predicting cue, cue conditioning would occur. However, if the stimulus is not serving as cue, contextual conditioning would increase (Baas et al., 2008).

We hypothesized cue conditioning to the distinct parts of the virtual environment, in which an US was administered in the conditioning phase. These cues only consisted of a certain moment in the situation in which a US has been applied before or not. As cues were not as distinct as in studies described earlier and here, the task to learn CS-US associations was more difficult for the participants. This could also be a reason why cue conditioning did not occur or at least could not be shown in recent study.

Moreover, the lack of cue conditioning could be caused by the association task for the participants. As the virtual environment represented a very complex context containing many details, stimuli might have been too complex to be processed in early cortical voltage changes. Therefore, the difficult task is another possibility, which could have been too difficult to memorize single screenshot categories even on an unconscious level.

4.5 No cue conditioning or inappropriate method?

Now, it is interesting to have a closer look at the analyzed ERP components and options why fear conditioning could not be shown. The P100 is a very early ERP component highly associated with selective attention (Junghöfer et al., 2001). Here, the very complex pictures could be a reason for similar P100 amplitudes for all screenshot categories. Certain features located in the virtual room and displayed on the screenshots could serve as eye-catcher and attract participants' attention stronger than in the acquisition phases, when subjects were guided through the office and objects appeared gradually by movement. As the eye-catching objects by early processing of the screenshots might not be the same features that were observed when an US was administered in the conditioning phase, the ERP component P100 that is prominent for attention is not able to represent a cue conditioning effect evoked by the pictures.

However, in comparison to the diploma thesis (Meyer-Heintze, 2011), the LPP represented a more promising ERP in regard to show cue conditioning. According to

Schupp et al. (2000) and Bradley et al. (2007), the late positive potential might be modulated by emotional relevance of the stimulus as well as picture composition. Emotionality as well as strong figure-ground contrasts evoked enhanced LPP amplitudes. According to the pilot study, picture properties were adjusted as each group of stimuli had the statistically same picture properties like entropy, brightness and subjective complexity. Consequently, differences in LPP amplitudes should exclusively depict the emotional relevance of the stimuli. However, visual inspection of the LPP in centro-parietal scalp regions revealed a poorly distinct ERP component in all screenshot categories. Additionally, no associations between any emotionality and the screenshots were depicted, not even on a contextual level comparing CXT+ and CXT-. A reason could be one-trial learning. On one hand, clear evidence for one-trial learning was pointed out by Bröckelmann et al. (2011) and Steinberg et al. (2011). On the other hand, these studies mainly investigated early components recorded by magnetoencephalography (MEG), which were evoked by auditory stimuli or pictures of faces. An effect of enhanced attention to stimuli with emotional affect compared to neutral ones even with few trial learning was seen in early stages of stimulus processing not exceeding 190 ms after stimulus onset. However, these investigations did not address the analysis of later components and consequently can only be transferred to the recent study with caution. As the screenshot stimuli used in recent study might be too complex for fast processing and simultaneous associating with emotional meaning, it might be difficult to find distinct processing of various screenshot categories in the late ERP components.

Another effect of the poorly distinct LPP component might be the stimulus complexity and additionally the big size of the stimuli on the powerwall. Schupp et al. (2000) investigated the motivational relevance of a stimulus depicted in the LPP component up to 750 ms after stimulus onset by presenting IAPS pictures. It seems hard to conclude that the short presentation time of the complex and large stimuli in the recent study is enough to build up emotional relevance for distinct screenshots. This might be another reason why no distinct amplitudes regarding to various screenshot categories occurred.

Besides, the most interesting ERP component analyzed was the EPN, because David Meyer-Heintze (2011) found a decreased amplitude for CXT+US compared to CXT+noUS and CXT-, but only for participants assigned to the group that associated the context with red carpet as dangerous and the office with green carpet as safety context. As in the present study the carpet color as well as the stimulus complexity were controlled, no different EPN amplitudes could be revealed. The first argument for the influence of colors in the contexts was already discussed and verified in a study by Wilson (1966). Here, he confirmed that red environments affect subject's behavior in terms of an increased arousal and excitement, whereas green environments are attributed with restful and relaxing behavior. Consequently, greater alertness and attention during the observation of red environments could have caused the effect of an enhanced negative EPN for CXT+US vs. CXT+noUS and CXT- in Meyer-Heintze's study (2011). The second aspect of stimulus complexity was already mentioned above. Bradley et al. (2007) showed the greatest influence of picture properties in the EEG signal up to 250 ms after stimulus onset. 2009, Bradley emphasized that this effect occurs even without emotional relevance of the stimulus. As in the recent study, the EPN was analyzed from 240-280 ms, the ERP component modulation due to stimulus complexity could not be excluded. Therefore, the adapted entropy, brightness and complexity levels in all groups of stimuli on the same level might be the reason that we did not find any amplitude differences between screenshot categories.

However, the EPN and P100 revealed a distinct main effect of electrode location and of hemisphere. An increased EGG signal over occipital compared to parietal electrodes is obvious as this cortex area is highly relevant for visual stimulus processing (e.g. Wieser, Mühlberger, Kenntner-Mabiala & Pauli, 2006; Wieser et al., 2010). Generally, enhanced ERP amplitudes in the right compared to the left hemisphere showed a stronger processing of emotionally relevant stimuli. Basically, evidence for the lateralization effect was provided by experiments in which participants displayed enhanced processing of emotional information in the right brain hemisphere compared to the left (e.g. Junghöfer et al., 2001; Schwarz, Davidson & Maer, 1975; Wieser et al., 2010).

All in all, cue conditioning cannot be excluded in this paradigm, but ERPs give no evidence about conditioning in this study design.

4.6 Contextual conditioning and anxiety disorders

Contextual conditioning provides a lot of information about the associative learning of US and a certain context. Skin conductance level, as a physiological indicator for arousal (Bradley, 2009), increases generally in the CXT+ compared to CXT-. Patients with anxiety disorders often fail to learn the association between a context and the US, so they show an increased general arousal, independent of standing in the anxiety or safety context (Lissek et al., 2005). Therefore, when testing anxiety patients in recent experimental design, increased fear reactions as well as less contingency awareness due to an enhanced general anxiety could be expected. Lissek et al. (2005) distinguished simple conditioning procedures from differential conditioning. The first describes a paradigm in which anxiety patients and healthy controls were conditioned to one CS. Anxiety disorder patients responded stronger to the conditioned stimulus than healthy controls. In differential conditioning, a CS- is created in addition to the CS+. The CS- is never presented in combination with a US and therefore serves as a safety signal. However, in comparison to healthy controls, anxiety disorder patients showed less differentiation between both stimulus categories in terms of an increased reaction to CS+ and CS-. Craske et al. (2009) discussed potential mechanisms that lead to hypersensitivity of patients suffering from anxiety. The first possibility for the strong reaction even to CS- could originate from reduced contingency awareness in anxiety patients. However, this doesn't seem to be the main reason since many studies collected data about the contingency awareness and revealed the same rating levels in healthy controls and patients (Lissek et al., 2005). Second, sensitization and a lack of habituation were reported as impaired functions of the fear system in anxiety disorder patients. Third, also greater stimulus generalization is shown in anxious individuals (Craske et al., 2009). Generalization was recently tested using a similar paradigm as in this experiment. In the acquisition the same virtual office rooms were used. The generalization effect was investigated by adding a third office into the virtual environment, which consisted half of the safety and half of the anxiety context. Participants scoring higher in the trait anxiety questionnaire should respond in startle like being in the anxiety context whereas lower anxious individuals were thought to react like being in the safety context (study in preparation by Estelle Leombruni, Department of Psychology I, University of Würzburg). Fourth, inhibitory fear mechanisms could be impaired, which in turn impairs extinction learning (Craske et al., 2009).

Concluding, the recent study showed contextual fear conditioning in healthy participants due to subjective ratings and physiological arousal measurements in terms of skin conductance level. Generally, anxiety was enhanced in CXT+ compared to CXT-. It would be interesting for future studies to test context conditioning in virtual reality also with a sample of anxiety disorder patients. Then, conclusions could be drawn about the impairment of associative learning mechanisms in any emotional contexts.

4.7 Limitations and future directions

No evidence for cue conditioning was given, though contextual fear conditioning was proven. Fear-relevant surroundings might have been more effective to create cue conditioning (Mineka & Öhman, 2002), however, even in offices strong associative learning could occur. Maren et al. (2013) described a very arousing situation when a person loses his or her job. The person might have been invited into the boss' office and therein been dismissed. Subsequently, the context as well as some contextual features might be highly associated with aversion and a feeling of extremely high arousal afterwards.

Furthermore, the recent paradigm provided several limitations. First, extinction already started in the acquisition phases during different trials. In extinction learning, the CS is presented without the US and consequently the conditioned response decreases gradually. In particular, here participants were guided 6 times through the anxiety context and perceived a total amount of 12 US stimuli at 12 different locations. As one CS-US association only occurred once and in the next trials the CS never again was presented with a US, extinction learning already began as the second acquisition trial in the anxiety context started. A second limitation, associated with the first aspect, is extinction in the test phase. Every screenshot was presented three times, the CS-US associations might have been present for the first few stimuli, but in later phases of EEG recordings, all conditioned CS-US associations might have been extinguished. However, analyzing only the first half of the presented stimuli separately, equal amplitudes were evoked. Third, a different number of stimuli in the screenshot categories (12 for CXT+US and CXT+noUS each and 24 for CXT-) were not optimal for EEG recordings.

For future investigations, it would be interesting to add skin conductance response (SCR) measurements also to the test phase as a further indicator for cue conditioning. Unfortunately, the inter-trial intervals need to last several seconds to build up a physiological response and also a habituation effect could occur. As ERPs did not reveal any results, SCR might not change the problem of capturing cue conditioning. A more promising modification might be the EEG recording method. Recently, a conditioning study conducted by Anna Kastner (manuscript in preparation) revealed the effect of a distractor when processing an anxiety or safety context. Here, steady-state visually evoked potentials (ssVEP) were used instead of ERPs to investigate electro-cortical activation. Applying this method, stimulus pictures are presented that flicker in a distinct frequency, which can be chosen previously between 3-40 Hz (Vialatte, Maurice, Dauwels & Cichocki, 2010). Via complex demodulations the carrier frequency can be determined and distinct amplitudes can be calculated as a response to stimuli presented in a certain frequency using fast-Fourier transformation. In Kastner's study, a context picture was presented in the background over 20 s and a distractor (grandfather clock or person) in some cases appeared in the foreground for 4 s. As both components flickered in different but particular frequencies, context and cue conditioning could clearly be distinguished by analyzing evoked amplitudes of context and distractor. Here the main advantage is the very long presentation time of the cues, which assures the holistic processing of the stimulus. In the present experimental paradigm, screenshots could also be presented in flickering mode to evoke ssVEP amplitudes and subsequently provide information about implicit cue conditioning in the participants.

Another possibility to investigate cue conditioning is extracting particular features of the contexts, in this case for example the wall pictures, since they can be easily selected and controlled. During contextual conditioning, US presentation could be minimized to scenes, whenever certain wall pictures appear in the observer's field of view. CS-US associations could be created and they could represent cues in the test phase. On one hand, these cues would be completely integrated in the virtual context during the acquisition phase, and on the other hand, they would depict distinct features of the room and thereby be less complex than recently used screenshots. Additionally, investigating phobias, these pictures could also depict aversive contents like spiders, which modulate not only CS-US associations, but also fear relevant cues in particular as the preparedness theory revealed (Seligman, 1970).

As results indicate no ERP differences during the processing of screenshots of different categories, it might be worth not only to compare anxiety and safety contexts, but to add a third context, which could be appetitive conditioned as a positive, rewarding context. Assuming that cue conditioning existed, but the effect of the used screenshots was very weak, this positive reinforcement might provide greater differences in ERP amplitudes evoked by a very positive and a very negative context, but the level of arousal might be the same and only decreased for the safety context.

However, brain imaging techniques like functional magnetic resonance imaging (fMRI) or positron emission tomography (PET) could also be applied to measure the activity of subcortical structures in the human brain. In order to differentiate contextual and cue conditioning, the models of fear and anxiety and its neural correlates can be applied. Hence, an activated amygdala indicates enhanced cued fear (Walker et al., 2003) as well as contextual anxiety (Alvarez et al., 2011), whereas an activated BNST would be caused by increased contextual anxiety (Walker et al., 2003). Moreover, according to the *dual representation model* by Rudy (2004), the hippocampus binds features into a conjunctive representation, whereas the amygdala processes single features and elicits behavioral responses. Transferring recent experimental paradigm into a neuroimaging study could be a next step to get information about the activated brain structures during fear conditioning.

4.8 Conclusions

All in all, this study gives clear evidence of contextual fear conditioning in virtual reality on the explicit levels of skin conductance as well as of ratings. However, cue conditioning to the screenshots cannot be confirmed nor refuted, as event-related brain potentials seemed not to be an appropriate method to assess the distinct processing of the selected cues. Neither on a contextual nor on a cue conditioning level, ERPs provided evidence for any experimental manipulation. From evolutionary perspective, there must exist a very distinct neuronal system, which helps not only identifying but also responding adequately to environmental threat, even on explicit as well as implicit level (Mineka & Öhman, 2002).

Joseph LeDoux described in his recent review (2012) about the emotional brain the concept of a survival circuit, which integrates emotion, motivation reinforcement and arousal. Survival circuits include at least: circuits involved in defense, maintenance of energy and nutrition supplies, fluid balance, thermoregulation and reproduction.

To conclude, the importance of fear and anxiety and the necessity of their contribution for survival seems out of question. However, overreactions to threatening stimuli and the misinterpretation of safety signals (Seligman, 1971) can lead to fear and anxiety disorders, which are still not fully understood. Especially the development and the differentiation between contextual and cue conditioning remain under debate. The recent study emphasizes the importance of controlling stimuli to be able to draw conclusions. Furthermore, the study highlights advantages of virtual environments and the stimulus presentation in natural size, but also the problems that are connected to complex visual stimuli. Using EEG as method to record cue conditioning is very new and has to be established, yet. Therefore, optimizing the experimental design and the EEG method to capture the cue conditioning signal is still required. Nevertheless, the recent study provides a lot of information about contextual conditioning in VR and a basis for further investigations that could help to understand fear and anxiety in the future.

5 References

Aguilar, L. A. (2003). Neuroscience of Pavlovian conditioning: a brief review. *Spanish journal of psychology*, *6*(2), 155-167.

Alheid, G. F., Beltramino, C. A., De Olmos, J. S., Forbes, M. S., Swanson, D. J., & Heimer, L. (1998). The neuronal organization of the supracapsular part of the stria terminalis in the rat: the dorsal component of the extended amygdala. *Neuroscience*, *84*(4), 967-996.

Alonso, J., Angermeyer, M. C., Bernert, S., Bruffaerts, R., Brugha, T. S., Bryson, H., ... & Vollebergh, W. A. M. (2004). Sampling and methods of the European Study of the Epidemiology of Mental Disorders (ESEMeD) project. *Acta Psychiatrica Scandinavica*, *109*(420), 8-20.

Alpers, G. W. & Pauli, P. (2002). *Angstsensitivitäts-Index*. Würzburg: PsychScience.

Alvarez, R. P., Biggs, A., Chen, G., Pine, D. S., & Grillon, C. (2008). Contextual fear conditioning in humans: cortical-hippocampal and amygdala contributions. *The Journal of Neuroscience*, *28*(24), 6211-6219.

Alvarez, R. P., Chen, G., Bodurka, J., Kaplan, R., & Grillon, C. (2011). Phasic and sustained fear in humans elicits distinct patterns of brain activity. *Neuroimage*, *55*(1), 389-400.

American Psychiatric Association (1994). *Diagnostic and Statistical Manual of Mental Disorders, Fourth Edition*. Washington, DC: American Psychiatric Association.

Andreatta, M. (2010). *Emotional reactions after event learning: a Rift between Implicit and Explicit Conditioned Valence in Humans Pain Relief Learning* (Dissertation). Retrieved from http://opus.bibliothek.uni-wuerzburg.de/

Andreatta, M., Mühlberger, A., Yarali, A., Gerber, B., & Pauli, P. (2010). A rift between implicit and explicit conditioned valence in human pain relief learning. *Proceedings of the Royal Society B: Biological Sciences*, *277*(1692), 2411-2416.

Baas, J. M., Nugent, M., Lissek, S., Pine, D. S., & Grillon, C. (2004). Fear conditioning in virtual reality contexts: a new tool for the study of anxiety. *Biological psychiatry*, *55*(11), 1056-1060.

Baas, J. M. P., Van Ooijen, L., Goudriaan, A., & Kenemans, J. L. (2008). Failure to condition to a cue is associated with sustained contextual fear. *Acta psychologica*, *127*(3), 581-592.

Barrett, J., & Armony, J. L. (2009). Influence of trait anxiety on brain activity during the acquisition and extinction of aversive conditioning. *Psychological medicine*, *39*(02), 255-265.

Bear, M. F., Connors, B. W., Paradiso, M. A. (Eds.) (2007). *Neuroscience: exploring the brain*. Wolters Kluwer Health.

Bechara, A., Tranel, D., Damasio, H., Adolphs, R., Rockland, C., Damasio, A. R. (1995). Double Dissociation of Conditioning and Declarative Knowledge Relative to the Amygdala and Hippocampus in Humans, Science, 269, 1115-1118.

Berger, H. (1929). Über das elektrenkephalogramm des menschen. *European Archives of Psychiatry and Clinical Neuroscience*, *87*(1), 527-570.

Blanchard, R. J., & Blanchard, D. C. (1969). Crouching as an index of fear. *Journal of comparative and physiological psychology*, *67*(3), 370.

Blanchard, R. J., Yudko, E. B., Rodgers, R. J., & Blanchard, D. C. (1993). Defense system psychopharmacology: an ethological approach to the pharmacology of fear and anxiety. *Behavioural Brain Research*, *58*(1), 155-165.

Bohil, C. J., Alicea, B., & Biocca, F. A. (2011). Virtual reality in neuroscience research and therapy. *Nature reviews neuroscience*, *12*(12), 752-762.

Bolles, R. C. (1970). Species-specific defense reactions and avoidance learning. *Psychological review*, *77*(1), 32.

Bolles, R. C., & Fanselow, M. S. (1980). A perceptual-defensive-recuperative model of fear and pain. *Behavioral and Brain Sciences*, *3*(2), 291-301.

Bradley, M. M. (2009). Natural selective attention: Orienting and emotion. *Psychophysiology*, *46*(1), 1-11.

Bradley, M. M., Hamby, S., Löw, A., & Lang, P. J. (2007). Brain potentials in perception: picture complexity and emotional arousal. *Psychophysiology*, *44*(3), 364-373.

Bradley, M. M., Lang, P. J., & Cuthbert, B. N. (1993). Emotion, novelty, and the startle reflex: habituation in humans. *Behavioral neuroscience*, *107*(6), 970.

Bröckelmann, A.-K., Steinberg, C., Elling, L., Zwanzger, P., Pantev, C., & Junghöfer, M. (2011). Emotion-associated tones attract enhanced attention at early auditory processing: Magnetoencephalographic correlates. Journal of Neuroscience, 31(21), 7801-7810.

Carlsson, K., Andersson, J., Petrovic, P., Petersson, K. M., Öhman, A., & Ingvar, M. (2006). Predictability modulates the affective and sensory-discriminative neural processing of pain. Neuroimage, 32(4), 1804-1814.

Carver, C. S., & White, T. L. (1994). Behavioral inhibition, behavioral activation, and affective responses to impending reward and punishment: The BIS/BAS scales. Journal of Personality and Social Psychology, 67(2), 319-333.

Castellucci, V. F., & Kandel, E. R. (1974). A quantal analysis of the synaptic depression underlying habituation of the gill-withdrawal reflex in Aplysia. Proceedings of the National Academy of Sciences, 71(12), 5004-5008.

Chan, C. K., & Lovibond, P. F. (1996). Expectancy bias in trait anxiety. Journal of Abnormal Psychology, 105(4), 637.

Craske, M. G., Rauch, S. L., Ursano, R., Prenoveau, J., Pine, D. S., & Zinbarg, R. E. (2009). What is an anxiety disorder?. Depression and Anxiety, 26(12), 1066-1085.

Cuthbert, B. N., Schupp, H. T., Bradley, M. M., Birbaumer, N., & Lang, P. J. (2000). Brain potentials in affective picture processing: covariation with autonomic arousal and affective report. Biological psychology, 52(2), 95-111.

Davis, M., Walker, D. L., Miles, L., & Grillon, C. (2009). Phasic vs sustained fear in rats and humans: role of the extended amygdala in fear vs anxiety. Neuropsychopharmacology, 35(1), 105-135.

Elliot, A. J., Maier, M. A., Binser, M. J., Friedman, R., & Pekrun, R. (2009). The effect of red on avoidance behavior in achievement contexts. Personality and Social Psychology Bulletin, 35(3), 365-375.

Elliot, A. J., & Niesta, D. (2008). Romantic red: red enhances men's attraction to women. Journal of personality and social psychology, 95(5), 1150.

Fanselow, M. S. (1984). What is conditioned fear? Trends in Neurosciences, 7(12), 460-462.

Fanselow, M. S. (1990). Factors governing one-trial contextual conditioning. *Animal Learning & Behavior, 18*(3), 264-270.

Fanselow, M. S. (1994). Neural organization of the defensive behavior system responsible for fear. *Psychonomic Bulletin & Review, 1*(4), 429-438.

Fenz, W. D., & Epstein, S. (1967). Gradients of physiological arousal in parachutists as a function of an approaching jump. *Psychosomatic Medicine, 29*(1), 33-51.

Freire, R. C., De Carvalho, M. R., Joffily, M., Zin, W. A., & Nardi, A. E. (2010). Anxiogenic properties of a computer simulation for panic disorder with agoraphobia. *Journal of affective disorders, 125*(1), 301-306.

Glotzbach-Schoon, E., Tadda, R., Andreatta, M., Tröger, C., Ewald, H., Grillon, C., ... & Mühlberger, A. (2013). Enhanced discrimination between threatening and safe contexts in high-anxious individuals. *Biological psychology, 93*, 159-166.

Gratton, G., Coles, M. G., & Donchin, E. (1983). A new method for off-line removal of ocular artifact. *Electroencephalography and clinical neurophysiology, 55*(4), 468-484.

Grillon, C. (2002). Startle reactivity and anxiety disorders: aversive conditioning, context, and neurobiology. *Biological psychiatry, 52*(10), 958-975.

Grillon, C. (2008). Models and mechanisms of anxiety: evidence from startle studies. *Psychopharmacology, 199*(3), 421-437.

Grillon, C., Baas, J. M., Cornwell, B., & Johnson, L. (2006). Context conditioning and behavioral avoidance in a virtual reality environment: effect of predictability. *Biological psychiatry, 60*(7), 752-759.

Grillon, C., Cordova, J., Morgan III, C. A., Charney, D. S., & Davis, M. (2004). Effects of the beta-blocker propranolol on cued and contextual fear conditioning in humans. *Psychopharmacology, 175*(3), 342-352.

Grillon, C., & Davis, M. (1997). Fear-potentiated startle conditioning in humans: Explicit and contextual cue conditioning following paired versus unpaired training. *Psychophysiology, 34*(4), 451-458.

Günther, A. C., Bottai, M., Schandl, A. R., Storm, H., Rossi, P., & Sackey, P. V. (2013). Palmar skin conductance variability and the relation to stimulation, pain and the motor activity assessment scale in intensive care unit patients. *Critical Care, 17*(2), R51.

Hamm, A. O., & Weike, A. I. (2005). The neuropsychology of fear learning and fear regulation. *International Journal of Psychophysiology*, *57*(1), 5-14.

Handy, T. C. (Ed.). (2005). *Event-related potentials: A methods handbook*. The MIT Press.

Hasler, G., Fromm, S., Alvarez, R. P., Luckenbaugh, D. A., Drevets, W. C., & Grillon, C. (2007). Cerebral blood flow in immediate and sustained anxiety. *The Journal of neuroscience*, *27*(23), 6313-6319.

Hillyard, S. A., & Münte, T. F. (1984). Selective attention to color and location: An analysis with event-related brain potentials. *Perception & Psychophysics*, *36*(2), 185-198.

Hillyard, S. A., Vogel, E. K., & Luck, S. J. (1998). Sensory gain control (amplification) as a mechanism of selective attention: electrophysiological and neuroimaging evidence. *Philosophical Transactions of the Royal Society of London. Series B: Biological Sciences*, *353*(1373), 1257-1270.

Hoffman, H. G., Richards, T. L., Bills, A. R., Van Oostrom, T., Magula, J., Seibel, E. J., & Sharar, S. R. (2006). Using fMRI to study the neural correlates of virtual reality analgesia. *CNS Spectr*, *11*(1), 45-51.

http://www.adaa.org/about-adaa/press-room/facts-statistics (08/20/2013).

Huff, N. C., Zielinski, D. J., Fecteau, M. E., Brady, R., & LaBar, K. S. (2010). Human fear conditioning conducted in full immersion 3-dimensional virtual reality. *Journal of visualized experiments: JoVE*, (42).

Hugdahl, K., & Johnsen, B. H. (1989). Preparedness and electrodermal fear-conditioning: Ontogenetic vs phylogenetic explanations. *Behaviour research and therapy*, *27*(3), 269-278.

Hurley, L. M., Devilbiss, D. M., & Waterhouse, B. D. (2004). A matter of focus: monoaminergic modulation of stimulus coding in mammalian sensory networks. *Current opinion in neurobiology*, *14*(4), 488-495.

Jackson, E. D., Payne, J. D., Nadel, L., & Jacobs, W. J. (2006). Stress differentially modulates fear conditioning in healthy men and women. *Biological psychiatry*, *59*(6), 516-522.

Junghöfer, M., Bradley, M. M., Elbert, T. R., & Lang, P. J. (2001). Fleeting images: A new look at early emotion discrimination. *Psychophysiology*, *38*(2), 175-178.

Kappeler-Setz, C., Gravenhorst, F., Schumm, J., Arnrich, B., & Tröster, G. (2013). Towards long term monitoring of electrodermal activity in daily life. *Personal and Ubiquitous Computing, 17*(2), 261-271.

Krohne, H. W., Egloff, B., Kohlmann, C.-W., Tausch, A. (1996). Untersuchungen mit einer deutschen Version der "Positive and negative Affect Schedule" (PANAS). *Diagnostica, 42,* 139-156.

Lang, P. J. (1995). The emotion probe: Studies of motivation and attention. *American psychologist, 50*(5), 372.

Lang, P. J., Bradley, M. M., & Cuthbert, B. N. (1999). *International Affective Picture System: Instruction manual and affective ratings.* Technical Report A-4, The Center for Research in Psychophysiology, University of Florida.

Lang, P. J., Davis, M., & Öhman, A. (2000). Fear and anxiety: animal models and human cognitive psychophysiology. *Journal of affective disorders, 61*(3), 137-159.

Laux, L., Glanzmann, P., Schaffner, P., & Spielberger, C. D. (1981). *State-Trait-Angstinventar (STAI).* Weinheim: Beltz.

LeDoux, J. E. (2000). Emotion circuits in the brain. *Annual review of neuroscience, 23*(1), 155-184.

LeDoux, J. (2012). Rethinking the emotional brain. *Neuron, 73*(4), 653-676.

Lissek, S., Powers, A. S., McClure, E. B., Phelps, E. A., Woldehawariat, G., Grillon, C., & Pine, D. S. (2005). Classical fear conditioning in the anxiety disorders: a meta-analysis. *Behaviour research and therapy, 43*(11), 1391-1424.

Luck, S. J., Woodman, G. F., & Vogel, E. K. (2000). Event-related potential studies of attention. *Trends in cognitive sciences, 4*(11), 432-440.

Lykken, D. T., & Venables, P. H. (1971). Direct measurement of skin conductance: A proposal for standardization. *Psychophysiology, 8*(5), 656-672.

Maltby, N., Kirsch, I., Mayers, M., & Allen, G. J. (2002). Virtual reality exposure therapy for the treatment of fear of flying: A controlled investigation. *Journal of Consulting and Clinical Psychology, 70*(5), 1112.

Maren, S., Phan, K. L., & Liberzon, I. (2013). The contextual brain: implications for fear conditioning, extinction and psychopathology. *Nature Reviews Neuroscience, 14*(6), 417-428.

Marschner, A., Kalisch, R., Vervliet, B., Vansteenwegen, D., & Büchel, C. (2008). Dissociable roles for the hippocampus and the amygdala in human cued versus context fear conditioning. *The Journal of Neuroscience, 28*(36), 9030-9036.

Matsumoto, Y., Menzel, R., Sandoz, J. C., & Giurfa, M. (2012). Revisiting olfactory classical conditioning of the proboscis extension response in honey bees: a step towards standardized procedures. *Journal of Neuroscience Methods, 211*, 159-167.

Mehta, R., & Zhu, R. J. (2009). Blue or red? Exploring the effect of color on cognitive task performances. *Science, 323*(5918), 1226-1229.

Meyer-Heintze, D. (2011). *Kontextkonditionierung in virtualler Realität und ihre hirnelektrischen Korrelate.* Diploma thesis at the Department of Psychology I, Julius-Maximilians-Universität Würzburg, unpublished.

Mineka, S. (1979). The role of fear in theories of avoidance learning, flooding, and extinction. *Psychological Bulletin, 86*(5), 985.

Mineka, S., & Öhman, A. (2002). Phobias and preparedness: The selective, automatic, and encapsulated nature of fear. *Biological Psychiatry, 52*(10), 927-937.

Mowrer, O. H., & Aiken, E. G. (1954). Contiguity vs. drive-reduction in conditioned fear: temporal variations in conditioned and unconditioned stimulus. *The American journal of psychology, 67*(1), 26-38.

Mühlberger, A., Wiedemann, G., Herrmann, M. J., & Pauli, P. (2006). Phylo-and ontogenetic fears and the expectation of danger: Differences between spider-and flight-phobic subjects in cognitive and physiological responses to disorder-specific stimuli. *Journal of Abnormal Psychology, 115*(3), 580.

Mühlberger, A., Wieser, M. J., Herrmann, M. J., Weyers, P., Tröger, C., & Pauli, P. (2009). Early cortical processing of natural and artificial emotional faces differs between lower and higher socially anxious persons. *Journal of neural transmission, 116*(6), 735-746.

Öhman, A., & Soares, J. J. (1994). " Unconscious anxiety": phobic responses to masked stimuli. *Journal of abnormal psychology, 103*(2), 231.

Öhman, A. (2009). Of snakes and faces: An evolutionary perspective on the psychology of fear. *Scandinavian journal of psychology, 50*(6), 543-552.

O'Reilly, R. C., & Rudy, J. W. (2001). Conjunctive representations in learning and memory: principles of cortical and hippocampal function. *Psychological review, 108*(2), 311.

Orr, S. P., & Roth, W. T. (2000). Psychophysiological assessment: clinical applications for PTSD. *Journal of affective Disorders, 61*(3), 225-240.

Pavlov, I. P. (1927). Conditioned reflex: An investigation of the physiological activity of the cerebral cortex. Translated and Edited by G. V. Anrep. London: Oxford University Press.

Picton, T. W., Bentin, S., Berg, P., Donchin, E., Hillyard, S. A., Johnson, R., ... & Taylor, M. J. (2000). Guidelines for using human event-related potentials to study cognition: Recording standards and publication criteria. *Psychophysiology, 37*(2), 127-152.

Reiss, S., Peterson, R., Gursky, D. M., & McNally, R. J. (1986). Anxiety sensitivity, anxiety frequency and the prediction of fearfulness. *Behaviour Research and Therapy, 24(1),* 1-8.

Rescorla, R. A. (1988). Pavlovian conditioning: It's not what you think it is. *American Psychologist, 43*(3), 151.

Rhudy, J. L., Bartley, E. J., & Williams, A. E. (2010). Habituation, sensitization, and emotional valence modulation of pain responses. *Pain, 148*(2), 320-327.

Rhudy, J. L., & Meagher, M. W. (2000). Fear and anxiety: divergent effects on human pain thresholds. *Pain, 84*(1), 65-75.

Roozendaal, B., McEwen, B. S., & Chattarji, S. (2009). Stress, memory and the amygdala. *Nature Reviews Neuroscience, 10*(6), 423-433.

Rudy, J. W., Huff, N. C., & Matus-Amat, P. (2004). Understanding contextual fear conditioning: insights from a two-process model. *Neuroscience & Biobehavioral Reviews, 28*(7), 675-685.

Rudy, J. W., & O'Reilly, R. C. (1999). Contextual fear conditioning, conjunctive representations, pattern completion, and the hippocampus. *Behavioral neuroscience, 113*(5), 867.

Rugg, M. D. & M. G. H. Coles (Eds.). *Electroencephalography of mind: Event-related brain potentials and cognition*. New York: Oxford University Press.

Schupp, H. T., Cuthbert, B. N., Bradley, M. M., Cacioppo, J. T., Ito, T., & Lang, P. J. (2000). Affective picture processing: the late positive potential is modulated by motivational relevance. *Psychophysiology, 37*(2), 257-261.

Schupp, H. T., Junghöfer, M., Weike, A. I., & Hamm, A. O. (2003). Attention and emotion: an ERP analysis of facilitated emotional stimulus processing. *Neuroreport, 14*(8), 1107-1110.

Schupp, H. T., Junghöfer, M., Weike, A. I., & Hamm, A. O. (2004). The selective processing of briefly presented affective pictures: An ERP analysis. *Psychophysiology, 41*(3), 441-449.

Schwartz, G. E., Davidson, R. J., & Maer, F. (1975). Right hemisphere lateralization for emotion in the human brain: Interactions with cognition. *Science, 190*(4211), 286-288.

Sehlmeyer, C., Schöning, S., Zwitserlood, P., Pfleiderer, B., Kircher, T., Arolt, V., & Konrad, C. (2009). Human fear conditioning and extinction in neuroimaging: a systematic review. *PloS one, 4*(6), e5865.

Seligman, M. E. (1968). Chronic fear produced by unpredictable electric shock. *Journal of Comparative and Physiological Psychology, 66*(2), 402.

Seligman, M. E. (1970). On the generality of the laws of learning. *Psychological review, 77*(5), 406.

Seligman, M. E. (1971). Phobias and preparedness. *Behavior therapy, 2*(3), 307-320.

Seligman, M. E., & Binik, Y. M. (1977). The safety signal hypothesis. *Pavlovian-operant interactions*, 165-187.

Spear, N. E. (1973). Retrieval of memory in animals. *Psychological Review, 80*(3), 163.

Spielberger, C., Gorsuch, R. L., & Lushene, R. E. (1970). *Manual for the State-Trait Anxiety Inventory*. Palo Alto, CA: Consulting Psychologists Press.

Squire, L. R. (1992). Memory and the hippocampus: a synthesis from findings with rats, monkeys, and humans. *Psychological review, 99*(2), 195.

Steinberg, C., Dobel, C., Schupp, H. T., Kissler, J., Elling, L., Pantev, C., & Junghöfer, M. (2011). Rapid and highly resolving: Affective evaluation of olfactorily conditioned faces. Journal of Cognitive Neuroscience, 1-11.

Strobel, A., Beaducel, A., Debener, S., & Brocke, B. (2001). Eine deutschsprachige Version des BIS/BAS-Fragebogens von Carver und White. *Zeitschrift für Differentielle und Diagnostische Psychologie, 22(3)*, 216-227.

Vialatte, F. B., Maurice, M., Dauwels, J., & Cichocki, A. (2010). Steady-state visually evoked potentials: focus on essential paradigms and future perspectives. *Progress in neurobiology, 90*(4), 418-438.

Viaud-Delmon, I., Warusfel, O., Seguelas, A., Rio, E., & Jouvent, R. (2006). High sensitivity to multisensory conflicts in agoraphobia exhibited by virtual reality. *European Psychiatry, 21*(7), 501-508.

Vuilleumier, P. (2005). How brains beware: neural mechanisms of emotional attention. *Trends in cognitive sciences, 9*(12), 585-594.

Walker, D. L., Toufexis, D. J., & Davis, M. (2003). Role of the bed nucleus of the stria terminalis versus the amygdala in fear, stress, and anxiety. *European journal of pharmacology, 463*(1), 199-216.

Watson, D., Clark, L. A., Tellegen, A. (1988). Development and Validation of Brief Measures of Positive and Negative Affect: The PANAS Scales. *Journal of Personality and Social Psychology, 54*, 1063-1070.

Wessa, M., Kanske, P., Neumeister, P., Bode, K., Heissler, J., & Schönfelder, S. (2010). EmoPicS: Subjektive und psychophysiologische Evaluation neuen Bildmaterials für die klinisch-biopsychologische Forschung. *Zeitschrift für Klinische Psychologie und Psychotherapy, Supplementum 1/11*, 77.

Wickelgren, W. A. (1979). Chunking and consolidation: A theoretical synthesis of semantic networks, configuring in conditioning, SR versus cognitive learning, normal forgetting, the amnesic syndrome, and the hippocampal arousal system. *Psychological Review, 86*(1), 44.

Wieser, M. J., Mühlberger, A., Kenntner-Mabiala, R., & Pauli, P. (2006). Is emotion processing affected by advancing age? An event-related brain potential study. *Brain Research, 1096*(1), 138-147.

Wieser, M. J., Pauli, P., Reicherts, P., & Mühlberger, A. (2010). Don't look at me in anger! Enhanced processing of angry faces in anticipation of public speaking. *Psychophysiology, 47(2),* 271-280.

Wilson, G. D. (1966). Arousal properties of red versus green. *Perceptual and motor skills, 23*(3), 947-949.